21 Po

Reiki

Abhishek Thakore
and
Usha Thakore

PUSTAK MAHAL®
Delhi • Bangalore • Mumbai • Patna • Hyderabad

Publishers

Pustak Mahal®, Delhi

J-3/16 , Daryaganj, New Delhi-110002
☎ 23276539, 23272783, 23272784 • *Fax:* 011-23260518
E-mail: info@pustakmahal.com • *Website:* www.pustakmahal.com

Sales Centre
10-B, Netaji Subhash Marg, Daryaganj, New Delhi-110002
☎ 23268292, 23268293, 23279900 • *Fax:* 011-23280567
E-mail: rapidexdelhi@indiatimes.com

Branch Offices
Bangalore: ☎ 22234025 • *Telefax:* 22240209
E-mail: pmblr@sancharnet.in • pustak@sancharnet.in
Mumbai: ☎ 22010941
E-mail: rapidex@bom5.vsnl.net.in
Patna: ☎ 3294193 • *Telefax:* 0612-2302719
E-mail: rapidexptn@rediffmail.com
Hyderabad: *Telefax:* 040-24737290
E-mail: pustakmahalhyd@yahoo.co.in

© **Pustak Mahal, Delhi**

ISBN 978-81-223-0825-9

Edition : 2008

The Copyright of this book, as well as all matter contained
herein (including illustrations) rests with the Publishers. No
person shall copy the name of the book, its title design,
matter and illustrations in any form and in any language,
totally or partially or in any distorted form. Anybody doing
so shall face legal action and will be responsible for damages.

Printed at : Aadi Printech, Delhi

Preface

As the undisputed leader of New Age therapies, Reiki has emerged as the primary energy for global transformation and personal mastery. Never before have so many people been able to access these subtle energies at the same time. It is for the first time that mankind has evolved to an age where the critical mass is all set to bring about global transformation.

Reiki, though popular, has been taught at the very basic level. In a general workshop for any level, only an attunement is passed and the practice is done. This is definitely sufficient, but the application of the wonderful Reiki energy is not completely taught – thus the view that Reiki only heals diseases. It can do much more and there are specific ways by which higher energies can be channelled for our specific purposes.

A doctor is trained not only about human anatomy but about the various tools that he will have to use as well. Similarly, in Reiki it is essential to learn and then use the plethora of tools available. In fact, we must learn to play around with Reiki – apply Reiki to anything and everything. The results are astonishing. Just like water takes the shape of any vessel it enters, Reiki starts working at any application.

At the Thakore Centre, we had numerous experiments with Reiki and after many trials, we short-listed a few specific ways in which the use of Reiki was much more powerful. The intensity of Reiki is immeasurable, like that of our thoughts or emotions. Can you ever say you felt five units of anger or eight units of excitement? No! Likewise, Reiki depends on experience, and as you apply the practices in this book, you will be able to see for yourself the wonderful changes in your energy level.

21 Power Tools of Reiki is a collection of different methods and tools that make Reiki more effective. After almost five years of constant research, we present this book, which will make you a true warrior with tools for all occasions.

Just as a discipline like Karate is for channelling and focusing physical energy through *kathas*, these power tools will ensure a concentrated projection of the energy. In all its simplicity, Reiki flows wherever required. The power tools only concentrate the flow. When a problem is attacked from all sides, it is solved faster and the different lines of attack are these power tools. Use them and see the difference. The power is yours... Go for it!

–Abhishek Thakore

Contents

Acknowledgements

I would like to thank God for choosing me to be a channel for this wonderful wisdom to be passed on.

To my Reiki teachers Chandran and Rita Bhat – their teachings remain a constant source of inspiration.

My mother for her blessings and encouragement and my mother-in-law for the keen interest in all my activities. My husband, who's a friend, philosopher and guide. My son Abhishek, a master in the making, for helping me with this book. To my daughter Akanksha for her suggestions and support. And to my other relatives and friends for their support.

I am also grateful to the people who have a lot of resistance to learn Reiki, for it gave me a chance to realise that you can't change a person unless the person wants to change himself. I am grateful to the reader for giving me an opportunity to share my knowledge.

–Usha Thakore

On my part, I would like to thank my mother, for being a living expression of joy and life and for bringing love and bliss into our lives. My father, the balancing force in my life, but for whom I would have been a blind follower of many inappropriate beliefs without questioning. My sister Akanksha for being a wonderful friend, supporter, ardent student and a thoughtful critic too.

Thank also to other relatives, teachers, friends and well-wishers. To Mr Ram Avtar Gupta, for being such a wonderful supporter. To Mr S.K. Roy for the help and patience as I completed this book. And to every person at Pustak Mahal who has been responsible, directly or indirectly, for the publication of this book.

–Abhishek Thakore

ATTITUDE TOOLS

1. Gratitude
2. Giving
3. Present Moment Awareness
4. Intention
5. Detachment

ATTITUDE TOOLS

It's in the way you think and believe that you achieve. Reiki is no different – a certain set of mental attributes tremendously help the flow of Reiki. These set of tools are not exercises to be done but are like a mental posture that is to be assumed before commencing Reiki.

Due to all its influences, our mind has been driven away from these noble attitudes. So, initially it might be a little difficult to get into the required mental state. But with practice, and improving results, the benefits of attitude tools will become obvious.

Using attitude tools is like watering a plant at its roots – the effect, though not immediate, is long lasting and very effective. The exercises add a practical dimension to each tool – and ensure that the results are quantified too.

Another obvious benefit of these tools is that it does not require any materials, only your mind that is ever present. These tools empower your mind, which is the creator of intention. And ultimately, all that counts is your intention.

Attitude determines Altitude.

So let us explore attitude tools!

1

Gratitude

What is it?

A feeling of thankfulness can be called gratefulness. When you feed a dog, it shows its gratitude by wagging its tail. Elders express gratitude with blessings and infants with blissful laughter.

There are many things in life that we take for granted so often, without ever realising how important they are. Have you ever been in a hurry one morning, only to find your washbasin tap not working? That's perhaps when you realised for the first time how convenient it was to have the basin!

Even at this moment when you read this book, you will be able to recognise the fact that it has come to you because of so many factors. Not only us as the authors, but the paper supplier, the publisher, the light that you're reading under or the place – all gifts that you tend to take for granted. We need to be in gratitude all the time.

Even more dangerous is the way we take people around us for granted. The closer a person is to us, the ruder we can be, and more the liberties we take with him or her! Isn't it true? Most children realise the value of their parents only after they are no more.

When we received our training in gratitude, we found it very silly initially. We were made to go and thank our footwear – a very powerful exercise! But soon we realised that it is gratitude that is the basic requirement for Reiki.

Needless to say, *gratitude is a great attitude!*

How to use

Gratitude by itself is also very powerful. The idea behind using gratitude is to be grateful to all the things that you have all the time. And to remember to thank God for everything too!

When you establish the awareness of gratitude, you automatically tune yourself with universal energies. Our experiments show that even people who have not learnt Reiki can acquire healing powers and empower their intentions merely by gratitude.

Using gratitude simply means expressing gratitude to things, people and situations whenever you remember. You can start your day by expressing gratitude to what you have, and end your day by expressing gratitude to the events of the day.

Also, it is very important to use gratitude in the toughest situations – when you're entrapped by negative emotions like anger, fear or frustration. Counting the plus points at such times makes a BIG difference. So, let's BIG – Be In Gratitude!

Where to use

Everywhere! More specifically, use the gratitude tool while you're giving Reiki to someone you don't love unconditionally. When we give Reiki to people who have knowingly or unknowingly hurt us, we block the flow of energy, and shift focus on our thoughts about that person.

However, expressing gratitude just before starting Reiki will clear all such blocks. Also, you might be in an inappropriate state to channel the energy. Expressing gratitude puts you in the right frame of mind.

You can also ask the receiver to express gratitude to the things he feels he should. He should also express gratitude to you, and Reiki as energy. This simple activity will dramatically change results.

Effects and changes

❏ *Better flow of Reiki* – You will experience the higher flow of Reiki. Since there are no other distractions for the flow of energy, it will be focused and direct.

❏ *Faster healing* – Subsequently, in a state of gratitude, your mind will be in a relaxed state. This is ideal for quick healing, a scientifically proven fact.

❏ *Unconditional love* – Being in gratitude enhances your ability to love unconditionally. This will emotionally energise the recipient, who will recover faster.

❏ *Attitude shift* – You move to a positive attitude, and see the brighter side of things. This attitude shift by itself is very important, and focusing on the good only increases it.

How it works

Gratitude is basically a mental state that can be achieved by anybody. It's perhaps one of the attitude tools that are simpler than Reiki itself. Gratitude dissolves your internal blocks and opens up the channel of energy within you. What happens then is that you experience a renewed and fresh flow of Reiki energy.

Exercises

See Reiki Prayer (Page 93).

Expressing gratitude simply implies making a mental statement saying, "I am grateful to _____ for _____."

1. Expressing gratitude to your footwear is a very powerful exercise. We treat footwear as something too insignificant and small, till the day you get shoe bites! People have made such situations pleasant by expressing gratitude to their footwear. So get up at this very moment and express gratitude to your footwear.

2. Environment thanking. At any point of the day when you pause, especially during your breaks, express

gratitude to the things all around – the sun and the sky, or the AC in your room, the atmosphere and nature itself. Spend some time observing things around you and mentally thank each one for serving you. Experience increased energy.

3. One of the most important uses of gratitude is expressing gratitude to food. Just before you eat, silently thank God, the person who cooked the food and all those factors responsible for the food reaching you. You will notice that the food tastes much better this way.

4. Recollect the most unpleasant incident of your life. Now with a gratitude mindset, relive the scene in total detail. Find ten reasons to be grateful to the incident. Till you reach a certain number of reasons, keep replaying the scene mentally. In the end, thank the person concerned or the event for the occurrence.

5. Expressing gratitude to your body at least once in a day is a great lesson in self-love. You can rub your palms together till they are slightly warm and massage your body. Leave no part untouched, and as you touch each part, express gratitude.

6. Gratitude also gives you freedom from ego. So, express gratitude to all the people and events that were responsible for making you the wonderful person you are today. This will ensure that you are never under the false notion that you are the greatest! In the world of Reiki we are all equal.

With the first tool in your armoury, you have acquired the basic tool for Reiki. Gratitude is to Reiki what a key is to a car – a must to start it. So grab the key of gratitude and start Reiki – this time you'll drive the car, not push it!

EXPERIENCE JOURNAL

Tool Name:

_____

Possible situations where you can apply it:

_____

_____

_____

_____

My experiences with the Power Tool:

Date	Situation	Experience

Improvements that need to be made in my approach:

_____

_____

_____

_____

2

Giving

"It is in giving that we all receive..."
(From the hymn, *Make me a channel of your peace*)

What is it?

What is giving? It is simply the most powerful tool that we humans have. An apt saying that comes to mind when I talk about giving at seminars is:

God gives.... and forgives

Man gets.... and forgets!

Look around you. If you've read the previous chapter, you'll know there are innumerable things around you for which you need to be grateful. God has given you all these things. Not that God actually comes in the form that you worship Him and hands these things over to you – it is Him working through each one of us. So when your mother is cooking and giving you food, it's God working through her and feeding you. When a teacher is teaching you, it's God using that channel to teach you. You keep receiving all the time – do you realise that?

However, when you get something, someone else is also giving something – so the total of giving and receiving in this universe is nil. Every time you get something irrespective of whether you value it or not, there is someone behind that who is the giver. That's the law of the universe. In order to create a culture of giving in each one of us, the CRITICAL MASS must start giving.

Look at nature and you'll find the most convincing examples for the cause of giving. For a start, look at your own breathing pattern – the way you breathe. It is one inhalation followed by another exhalation. Sounds obvious? Now what would happen, if you say that you would only take in the air, not give it out? If you decide to only breathe in, you'd probably blow up like a balloon! Or more likely, you'd actually choke yourself. Do you know why? Because you're missing out on one of the very important principles of the universe – giving.

Another example also concerns our body. In nature, whatever doesn't flow, stagnates. What would happen if you tie a tourniquet around your hand or even a finger? The blood flow would stop and that part of the body would start creating problems. Because once it is stagnant, it begins to degenerate. That's why your heart keeps pumping – 24 hours a day, 7 days a week, as long as you are alive. In fact, the very reason you are alive is because of this flow!

Remember: *Anything stagnant will degenerate!*

When you look at water bodies, this difference is even more profound. Have you ever seen weeds or moss in a flowing river? Definitely not! Because it keeps flowing. But look at a pond – it's more likely to get encumbered, because it is stagnant and still.

What do you want to be like? The pond or the river? The answer is obvious. And if you want to be like the river, you will need to practise giving.

Before we move on to the topic of giving in detail, let me tell you something about the giving cycle. If you are like most people, you are not in the cycle. So you do not receive much of anything – wealth, health, wishes, blessings etc. On the other hand, because you don't receive much, you don't give as well. It's a stand-off you are facing right now – because you don't give subsequently, you do not receive anything! Do you see that you are caught in the vicious circle of not giving and not receiving either?

This stand-off has to end, and nature is a little stern in this regard. It will always want you to start. It must have given you so many times, but you must have accepted the gift, without giving anything in return. Don't forget that contracts without consideration are void! Similarly, when you don't give anything, the flow of things coming to you will turn into a trickle... and then you enter the vicious circle, which is dangerous.

It reminds me of the story of a Chinese boy who was adamant and stubborn. It was a cold night and this kid was sitting next to the stove all alone. He needed heat, and he had some firewood to put in the stove. "Why should I put the firewood in first? Shouldn't I receive the heat? Let the stove start giving heat, and then we shall see." He sat there for a few hours, shivering badly in the cold, but still waiting for the stove to start the heat cycle. It was only when his father came in and gently told him to be forgiving towards the stove and put in the firewood that the heat started coming!

What a foolish kid! I can almost read your thoughts. But do you realise that you are also like that kid – wanting to hold on to all that you have, and expecting more. Give up! In the end, none of us is going to take anything away from this world – what will ultimately count is how much you have given. And make sure you've given a lot!

On the beautiful act of giving, there's a chapter in my book *31 Days to a New You: Just for Today I Will Give and be Open to Receiving*.

Give, and thou shalt receive.

Look at the world around you – and you'll see that you've been almost brainwashed to want. To want more and more. Ads, commercials and the media have all made you believe that you can't be happy till you have that particular product or service. You've been made the wanting kid.

When I began studying economics, I read that 'human wants are unlimited'. Today I see the truth of that statement more than ever before. If a modern man gets Aladdin's lamp, his first wish will be some possession he doesn't have – like a car or a computer. For his second wish he may ask for a big home or a place of fame. But I'm sure that for the third wish, he will ask for three more wishes!

We've heard the cliché 'True joy lies in giving', but never really experienced it. If you were to, you'll see how true it is. Before going into details on the topic of giving, you need to understand how to give. That is an art in itself!

When you are giving, the most important thing is the intention behind the act – why are you giving? If the act of giving makes you feel at a loss, it is of no benefit. True giving is for joy – it is for understanding the needs of others and trying to fulfil them. When you give and feel happy thereafter, you will see what I mean.

India has been a land of generosity. King Harsha Vardhana once gave away his own jewellery and clothing when donating to the people! Then there was Karna, who would give whatever was asked for, and even gave his protective shield that had afforded him invincibility! Such is the greatness of giving.

You need to be a giver to experience that joy – and you can start right away. There are people all around you to whom you can give something or the other of lasting value. When you add value to their lives they will add value to yours. When you give, you receive.

This universe too operates on circulation – where there is no circulation, there is stagnation. Look at your own body, for example. It is constantly taking in oxygen and giving out carbon dioxide. Your blood is constantly flowing through you. If this flow were to be blocked, it would create problems within you. Tie a string tightly to one of your fingers and restrict the blood flow – it will soon get discoloured and cold. Over a period of time, it will lose all sensation too.

It is a universal law that anything that stagnates, degenerates. So also, you need to keep things circulating. What you give need not be expensive. Look at impoverished Sudama, who took three fistfuls of rice for his friend Lord Krishna. But he was giving nevertheless. It is the act itself that counts.

Forget the cost, the gift needn't be material too – it can merely be a thought. You can mentally pray for the person, or send him blessings. Even these are acts of giving.

When you give, you create a vacuum in you – and nature abhors a vacuum. So more will flow into your life. Tithe is a great way to keep the circulation of money going – it is a custom whereby Christians give 10 per cent of their earnings to the church. Start giving today and you will see the dynamic flow that you set in motion. Only ensure that when you give, you give with a grateful heart and an intention to benefit the other person.

The other component to giving is receiving. You will see that when you start giving, gifts will pour into your life too. One word of caution though – don't expect this to happen and give for this reason! However, when gifts do come your way, accept them gracefully. Be open to receiving too. Remember, such circulation will make you spiritually healthy too! There is more than enough for everyone in this universe.

How to use

1. Just for today, try to give to every person you come across. It can be anything small like a flower, or a chocolate, but try to give with a grateful heart.

2. If you can't give anything material, you can at least mentally pray for the person. Maybe you can give a compliment too.

3. Circulate wealth – be open to giving money. Do it with the intention of giving benefit to the other person, and not grudgingly.

4. Also be open to receiving gifts from the universe – everyone around you basically.

5. At the end of the day, list what you consciously gave and got. You'll be surprised!

Where to use

In giving Reiki, don't ever hesitate – just keep looking for openings – opportunities to give Reiki to people and things. At any point of time, you're sure to find people around you who seem to be unhappy. Start right away... express the gratitude and switch on the Reiki. If you're an experienced practitioner, you will see the changes soon.

Whenever we go to zoos, it is only to provide Reiki to animals there! Poor troubled animals that need help, because of some suffering or pain, respond wonderfully to Reiki. For best results, try a fishpond – the fish automatically come to you when you start the flow of Reiki.

A weeping child is another great experiment. Whenever you find a baby weeping uncontrollably, smile broadly, express gratitude and start! At times you'll find that the child actually stops weeping and begins playing with you!

Apart from giving Reiki, you can also cover the scene with white light (read the chapter on white light for more details on this).

Effects and changes

As you begin to give, you start a dynamic cycle of give and take, i.e. exchange, you create a vacuum in yourself. And as we mentioned, nature abhors a vacuum, and rushes in to fill it...

Coincidentally, the law of the universe rules that what you give is what you get, because that kind of energy is exchanged. When you think about it finally, it's all about energy, isn't it?

How it works

Giving basically works on the principle of energy exchange. In the common version of Mikao Usui's story, you will remember there was a time when Usui taught beggars free of charge. For a few days, the change lasted, but then, the beggars began to return. It happened this way because there was no energy exchange. The beggars did not give anything in return for Reiki. Usui generated the positive energy, but it did not last with the beggars, for they were not prepared to let go of anything.

Mikao Usui

If you look at the universe, it's a zero-sum game – so you automatically receive when someone is giving, and vice versa. So when you start giving, you begin the flow. A classic example is that of a juggler trying to juggle a number of objects – he has to throw an object so that his hands get free to catch another one. When you start giving, you become like the juggler – giving and receiving non-stop.

Exercises

1. *The compliment game.* In a room full of people, one person can start the game. The group can consist of strangers too, but it's much better if there are known people only. One person starts off by paying compliments to any two people in the room. The compliments must be genuine and from the heart. Maintain eye contact and, wherever possible, hold hands while paying the compliments.

   In turn, each person who receives the compliment has to compliment two other people. What we have then is a chain reaction of compliments. Each person who has received a pre-determined number of compliments may sit out of the game and let it continue. You will see the wonderful air of positivity after this game.

   Reiki masters can use this game in their workshops too.

2. *Giving for no reason.* Practise giving for no reason – just give anything, a gift or a prayer, everyday to one person. Similarly, before you sleep, send love and Reiki, blessings and healing to all your loved ones, your country and the world at large.

   After practice of a month or so, your experiences will dramatically change!

3. *Charity.* Tithing and charity are the best ways to keep your wealth circulating. We suggest a charity of 10% of your income – you can donate to a recognised charitable trust or to individuals in need. Where beggars are concerned, we suggest you use your discretion – if the person really appears to be needy, you could give alms.

4. *Letters.* You can start the cycle of giving by making constructive suggestions to people who would really care for it. Ensure the other person is receptive. The goal of letters is to give suggestions, and not criticise. For a start, why don't you write to us? The address is at the end of the book, so drop in your experiences and suggestions for the book.

   We will definitely reply, but hey! Don't expect it!

5. *Clearing the junk.* There are a number of things in your closet that you've stocked convincing yourself that you'll need it someday – just give it away! Things that aren't being used are clutter – and they clutter up your mind too. Ask around and you'll find that there are a number of people who will be willing to receive.

6. *Energy exchange.* If you really want the receiver to value Reiki, insist on energy exchange. You can let the person first understand the whole idea of giving. Do this by telling him Usui's story, and even reading this chapter. The energy exchange need not necessarily be monetary, though it is best given and received in monetary terms. You can ask the person to motivate somebody else to learn Reiki, or assist in some workshops and so on. But always remember to balance the energy, and insist on energy exchange.

EXPERIENCE JOURNAL

Tool Name:

_____

Possible situations where you can apply it:

_____

_____

_____

My experiences with the Power Tool:

Date	Situation	Experience

Improvements that need to be made in my approach:

_____

_____

_____

3

Present Moment Awareness

The past is history,
The future – a mystery,
But this moment is a gift....
So it is called "present".

What is it?

How wonderfully do these lines describe the essence of joyful living! One of the best ways of improving your healing energies, as well as being perpetually happy, is hidden in these words. Even if we follow this alone, our ability to give and receive Reiki will drastically change.

The mantra is: BE IN THE PRESENT. Enjoy this moment. Life is a journey where you are not sure of your destination. So why wait for the destination that is not even known, and leave our happiness to it? Let us enjoy the present. The journey of life itself. Why not forget our past guilts and future worries to enjoy the present moment and experience it to the fullest?

The mind is a machine programmed to misbehave. This happens most times, as our mind is out of our control. We cannot do what we ourselves feel, but are rather driven by the desires of the mind. Buddha said that between two men, one of whom had defeated a thousand armies and the other who had controlled his mind, the latter was much greater! Even a hero like Arjuna found it difficult to control his own mind, so great is the challenge of controlling the mind.

At the very first opportunity, the mind has a monkey-like tendency to jump either to the future or the past without any rhyme or reason. This flow of thoughts is beyond our control. We need to train our mind to be focused. Meditation helps a lot and the most common form of meditation has been described at the end of this chapter. However, if we are completely focused in doing the task of the present moment, every job can be a meditation in itself.

How easy it seems! Once we do this, not only will our life be entirely free of struggle, but every job will also be a joy and a work of art. Participate in any activity with total concentration and you will notice that the quality of work shows a marked improvement and we enjoy more satisfaction. Every task then becomes a meditation. It is the same with Reiki. Always remember to be into a task one hundred per cent – including giving Reiki. When you are healing, let the energies flow from your heart.

Another very important aspect of this law is the matching of your thoughts and actions. You might have expected a very positive result out of something, but in the end it turned out to be terrible. What went wrong? Didn't you align your thinking in a positive direction? Didn't you hope for the best? Then why did this happen?

This happened because your thoughts and actions didn't match. Once you have decided to do something, apply yourself to it fully. Leave no stone unturned to achieve it. Give your best shot to every game. This is not only for the Herculean tasks in your life but also for every small thing, like preparing tea, or playing a game. Likewise, when giving Reiki, let your thought be that the best will happen for the person. Bear no grudges, for it can have an adverse impact.

There is no hope in the future
where there is no power in the present

How to use

❏ The use of this tool lies in the simple act of centring yourself whenever your mind wanders. This can be accomplished in a number of ways.

❏ One of the best ways is to start focusing on your breathing. Take your entire attention on your breath as you start breathing deeply, and slowly. This will not only have a calming effect on your mind, but also get you into the NOW.

❏ Another way to do this is by the simple act of clapping! A loud clap can turn your attention onto the present moment when nothing else does.

❏ You can focus on your surroundings – observe very closely what is around you, and you will notice that objects, shapes and colours actually stand out. This is because you are coming into the present, getting more and more centred. This works even better when you're observing trees and natural beauty.

Where to use

Just before you give Reiki, if you can centre yourself in the present, it will have a drastic impact on the effectiveness to the patient. You need to centre yourself just before you start a particular Reiki session. How will you do this? By focusing on your breathing as you give Reiki. Also, during the prayer, shift all your attention to the patient, and project love on him/her.

Similarly, whenever you have to give distant Reiki, it becomes even more important to get centred so that you can project energy more effectively.

Generally too, it helps to stay focused in the present, so that you will get a general feeling of well-being. This will help you maintain a much higher energy level, all the time.

Effects and changes

You will see that as you get centred in the present, you are able to actually feel the flow of Reiki. This manifests differently in different practitioners. Some feel a tingling sensation in the palms. Others find their palms getting warm, while some find a cooling sensation. Our bodies respond differently to the same energy. It doesn't matter how your body responds, you'll be able to notice a difference in the way you feel Reiki flowing.

Another major change that you'll notice is that your patient becomes more receptive to Reiki – s/he will be able to receive energy much better, if you can actually focus your attention on him/her. You may wonder: how does this work? The answer lies in the complex activities that take place at the subtle level of the body and the mind. You just need to observe, rather than understand.

And, of course, the most obvious pay off of this whole process is that you maintain a high energy level and a general sense of well-being throughout. You will find people getting more drawn towards you, as you develop a presence. You will derive much more satisfaction from whatever you do, and nothing will appear to be boring, since interest is merely lack of focus on a subject.

How it works

Your jumping mind oscillates from the past to the future; in this, it wastes a lot of energy. The thoughts that come into your mind will always affect you on the physical plane too, due to the body-mind connection. Any discomfort in your body will mean that it will have to first restore its own energy level before it can be capable of providing Reiki energy.

However, when you focus in the present, that focus itself is a very powerful tool to bring your attention to the present moment. You will realise your energy also tends to flow with your attention – so when your attention is focused on the recipient of the energy, the effect is much better.

Exercises

1. *The clap game.* This game is a simple process to draw your attention into the present. One person is the host of the game who has to clap his hands. All the other players must try and coincide their clapping with that of the host. Once in a while, the host must not clap but just do the action. People who are already lost in thought or out of focus will still clap! A great way to train concentration.

2. *Waking up instantly.* Get up from your bed as soon as you are awake. The time you spend lazing on the bed results in waste of unnecessary mental energy, which results in a tired mind throughout the day. Again, at night you must go to bed only when you feel sleepy. Lying on the bed and thinking wildly is the most unproductive habit. Sleep with the surrender of all your worries to God.

3. *Watching your words.* Make a commitment to yourself at the beginning of every day to be in the present as much as possible. Decide not to speak to anyone of any past event. Soon this will become a habit and your life will no longer be a burden of the past or a fear of the future.

4. *Healing the past.* To ensure you don't dwell in the past, heal it. Your present is affected to a great extent by your past. Forgive yourself for all your mistakes. Remember, whatever you did at any given moment in the past was the best way you could do. So don't regret it.

Realise that the past and future are nothing but mere impressions on your brain, only traces of proteins that give you an altered sense of reality. Grasp this perspective, and you'll break free, and actually begin to live in the present!

EXPERIENCE JOURNAL

Tool Name:

_____

Possible situations where you can apply it:

_____

_____

_____

My experiences with the Power Tool:

Date	Situation	Experience

Improvements that need to be made in my approach:

_____

_____

_____

4
Intention

What is it?

Simply speaking, intention is a thought that's held in the mind for a particular outcome. If you look at any creation, you will see that it is created twice – once in the mind of the creator, and then, in reality. Intention is merely the process of creating the result that you desire in your mind first.

Intent is a mental posture, a state of mind about a particular outcome. And your mind, which is connected to your cosmic computer, attracts anything that is held as an intention in it. If you look at your current life situation, realise that you have mentally attracted it to yourself. You have held the picture of this situation in front of you, consciously or subconsciously.

Let me clarify further. Even if you face an inevitable problem, by having a strong conviction that the problem will be solved, you will contribute greatly to that effect. The universe, bcth spiritually and scientifically, is nothing but energy and information. And this energy responds beautifully to your convictions and intentions.

Likewise, when you give Reiki or hold a positive intention about the well-being of your patient, the response of the receiver is much better.

How to use

Expressing intentions mentally

Just before you start a session of Reiki, mentally express an intention for the well-being of the person. Let it be an affirmation that you repeat thrice before starting to give Reiki.

Visualisation

When providing Reiki, it helps a lot if you visualise that part as healed. You can also visualise white light healing that area. Either way, the effect of visualisation is to crystallise your intent.

Intentional Reiki

Beyond a point of Reiki practice, you will reach a situation where Reiki will flow merely at your will or intention. This technique is often taught in Karuna Reiki too. Once you see something or somebody that needs Reiki, mentally focus on the well-being of the person. Express gratitude and the Reiki will be switched on.

Where to use

Intention is nothing but a mental posture – so it can be assumed all the time. Whenever you are aware of your thoughts, bear this positive intention in your mind, for all that you desire. You can hold an intention for the well-being of your people, your community and the world at large.

Even the situations that countries and societies are in happen to be nothing but a result of their own collective intentions. So when even one member of society holds a positive intention, he contributes to the collective thought pool. When more than one person does this, what you are effectively doing is generating a thought wave in the cosmic consciousness. Nature shall manifest this using all that it has.

New Age gurus have been able to cure cancer when they strongly held the intention of recovery, and made the patient hold the same intention too. That's the miracle of intention. It is like a signboard that your mind will constantly read, and therefore create for real.

As a mental posture, it is possible to keep an intention for all that you want to change and improve in life. It can be your finances, your relationships, studies or concentration. Basically anything that you think must improve. Just mentally wish that this should happen and it will. You never know when God will be reading your mind!

Effects and changes

You will see that with the use of intention, slowly but surely things start to change. Anything is always created twice, first in the mind and then in reality. Pick up any invention, any theory, any achievement. It has always happened first in the mind of the conceiver and then in reality. When you have an intention, things will start to change.

Now there is no guarantee as to which way things will change! There may be times when the exact opposite of what you had intended happens! Isn't that too risky? However, do not worry. As you continue on your path of regular practice of Reiki, your intention will become more and more powerful. It is only a question of how well you can communicate to your subconscious mind, and how detached you are. There are more chapters dedicated to this concept.

As of now, if you have still not done the 21 days' practice, do it right away. Start it, because it is only after this that your intentions will become empowered. Praying to Reiki energy, and holding intentions in your mind when you give Reiki, also help a lot.

How it works

The acid test of intention is faith. During your journey as a Reiki practitioner and seeker, there will be many times when things that you never intended happen.

During my SSC exams, for instance, I used all possible ways to avoid getting the Sulphur Dioxide experiment – and what I got was exactly that. How could this happen to me? Having just started on the path, this was a rare failure (as you spend more time using intention, you will realise that it always doesn't happen that way).

However, what you need to realise here is that God has a better plan for you – a better idea or a better thought.

31

There are times, there are days,
Days and months we cannot see God's ways,
Months and days we fail to scan,
What is His eternal plan,
But we still know that He can,
In His way.
(*From the hymn,* In His time)

This is where you need to remember that after you have tried your best, you have to leave the rest to God.

Another issue with intentions is that they really take time to manifest. Living in this instant world, we have begun to expect everything to happen or work instantly – but it is never so with the best things. It takes nine months to deliver a baby. It took over 20 years to build the Taj Mahal. Likewise, the best things take time. You just need to have faith that it will come to pass, some time or the other. The seed will sprout into a tree when the season is right.

Do not ever give up on your intention, as long as you want it. Keep it with you, for you never know when it will come to pass. It is important to introduce your intention in a quiet mind, where it shall connect with the cosmic computer.

It works like this – when you see the turbulent sea, nothing can make any difference to it. You can put the Qutub Minar in the sea and it will make no difference. Then, look at a quiet pond and you'll notice that even dropping a tiny pebble creates ripples. Compare this body of water to your mind. If your mind is as turbulent as the sea, this intention will have the status of a thought – it will make no measurable impact. But if it is dropped into the silent mind, there will be a series of events that will make it happen.

The principle of intention works on the power of your subconscious mind too – it is there that you drop your intentions. And the subconscious mind is connected to the mighty cosmic computer. It has the power to make the intention come true. So now, you know the secret of how intention works!

Exercises

1. ***Well-being intention.*** Whenever you are giving Reiki, at the top of your mind must be the intention of the total well-being of the person. If you do not have this intention, Reiki will not flow. So keep that mental intention even when you're giving Reiki to a stranger. Or an enemy!

2. ***Intentions for yourself.*** Always keep an intention that you must become a better Reiki healer – that way you will be contributing a lot to the growth of your own potential.

3. ***Intention list.*** Make a list of all your intentions on flash cards. Refer to it often, so that each time you do so, you mentally give energy to each and every intention.

4. ***Combining with other power tools.*** Remember that the best way to use power tools is in conjunction with each other. So also, intention is best used with affirmations, visualisations and, most importantly, detachment.

5. ***Acceptance.*** Whenever your intention does not happen, learn to accept it. Mentally say to God, "I love your roses, I love your thorns."

That was intention for you. Now harbour the intention that you begin to use it in your daily life. That will be your first intention!

EXPERIENCE JOURNAL

Tool Name:

_____

Possible situations where you can apply it:

_____

_____

_____

My experiences with the Power Tool:

Date	Situation	Experience

Improvements that need to be made in my approach:

_____

_____

_____

5

Detachment

"Do the karma, *don't bother about the* karmaphala.*"*
–Lord Krishna to Arjuna in the *Bhagavad Gita*

What is it?

Detachment is the essence of all spiritual practice and achievement. If there is one secret to effectiveness, one ingredient that most success recipes miss, it is Detachment. Lord Krishna exhorted Arjuna to be detached while performing his duty.

The whole idea of detachment is a part of most philosophies and traditions across the world. Yet, simple as it might seem, detachment is more difficult to attain than to understand. In your mind, on one end where you hold an intention, asking you to be detached is like asking you to do the reverse. But that is exactly the way it is. Consider a few examples.

Sheila had begun to meditate and learnt Reiki. All of a sudden, her life seemed to have changed. Mysterious happenings led her to higher awareness. She could actually feel that higher energy and she collected a group of like-minded people. They would meet once a week and share all their experiences. Her healing became all-powerful and many came to be healed by her. She decided that she was destined to be a Reiki Master.

Then one day, all of a sudden, all this stopped. Completely. Her happiness seemed to have vanished; the healing power was no longer there. She lost all sensitivity to energy. And Sheila slumped into depression. What went wrong?

When on the path of Reiki, one often tends to get enchanted by the numerous mystical experiences that life spontaneously seems to throw up. Suddenly, intuitive and mysterious messages start coming forth. Overnight, you become a healer and begin to believe that you have a special gift of God that others don't. As a result, we feel we are finally close to the Ultimate Divine. Then, the inevitable happens. All of a sudden, the experiences stop. And often, we try to find what is wrong with life. Why have we suddenly stopped experiencing the Divine Bliss?

There may be many reasons for this. You may have come into contact with a negative person. You may have had a negative thought, which took your mental energy and manifested itself. But the primary and root cause for all this is attachment.

I clearly recall telling my friend: "I take my life as a game, game after game. You take this game as your life."

He asked, "How is it that you always win?"

I intuitively replied, "I'm not bothered about the result, only about my performance. The result takes care of itself."

Thus, attachment is an increased botheration with the result. It is a loss of trust in destiny, in Reiki energy itself. It is sometimes an absence of self-confidence that you would be able to bring about a healing, and at other times, feverishness about the result. That's when you equate the result with your self-esteem, asking: 'How can I not get this result?' That's the time when nature decides to teach you a lesson in humility.

How to use

When you are in regular practice with Reiki, your intentions become really powerful. You can make things happen and initially this appears to be very interesting, making you very powerful. But then the results stop coming and you feel depressed. This is because you have changed your intentions into desires. There are a few things that you have to keep in mind to stay on the "level".

Firstly, as a Reiki paradigm goes, your needs will be taken care of, not your desires. And the easiest way of making one's desire a need is to use the desired objective for someone else's development. Say, for example, I desire a book, which I somehow can't get. Then I realise that this knowledge would be useful not only for me but for this particular friend of mine too. So I must search for the book, not for me, but for him. And lo! I get the book. My desire became my need when I decided to use it for someone else's cause. As you progress spiritually, the universe pampers you. Your needs increase and they are easily fulfilled.

The next common mistake that seekers make is what I call the means-end mistake. We perceive the means as the end. And that's where the conflict starts. Say, for example, you desire a car, because you want to reach your workplace comfortably. You use all the techniques you know and try your best to manifest this intention of yours. Frustration creeps in when you realise that it is just not happening. What you have ignored in this wild chase of yours is that the new family that has just shifted into your locality has a friendly man who works next to your workplace. He offers you a car pool. See how beautifully the universe has solved your problem! You don't need to drive, you have a new friend and you're saving petrol and keeping the environment cleaner! But will you ever realise that if you are trying mainly for the car? The car is only the means; the end is your comfort. Look back and you will realise that most of your unmanifest desires were not ends but means.

Elaborating further, here is another common example. When you take a taxi, what do you tell the taxi driver? The destination you want to go, or the exact route you wish to take. Are you constantly telling the driver take this turn, now go here etc? No. You know the driver is an expert and you only have to tell him your destination. He'll take you there by the best route. And that route might be even better than the one you know. Similarly, the universe is an expert at manifesting your intentions. But it is important to choose your final goal and not stick to a rigid path to achieve it. There are numerous ways to go from point A to point B and the shortest distance might not be the best. So choose the destination, not the path. And once you choose your destination, you don't need to bother. The path will unfold magically. You just have to be aware.

Cynics might argue that many times they had decided the way it should happen and succeeded. But friends, have you realised the amount of energy you have wasted in sticking to that path. When a farmer sows seeds, does he dig up the ground everyday to see how well they have grown? No! If he did, the seeds would never ever grow up.

Where to use

Use detachment as a partner of intention – wherever you have an intention to achieve something, have detachment towards it too. Detachment comes from a sense of certainty that the best will happen. Remember that when you're on the path of Reiki, nothing wrong can ever happen to you. Have that childlike faith in God and you'll see that your detachment gets better.

Mainly when you get a really challenging case to heal, remember that one of the most important aspects of it is the person's own *karmas*, and there is no one who can change that. Maybe the person has to go through the suffering. You can't play God at such a time and try and cure. What you must do is try your best.

Thus, whenever you give Reiki to a person or a situation, have an intention that the best thing will happen. Do not desire that a particular thing take place.

A major dilemma also comes up when you're giving Reiki to a dying person – what should you have as an intention? You can't intend that the person must die! Neither can you see any scope of the person getting better. What should you do?

You must harbour an intention about the well-being of the person – let Reiki handle the details. Let your only intention be that whatever is the best for the person must come to pass. Leave the rest to destiny. It shall be so.

Effects and changes

Call detachment the supreme law – for you will see that because of detachment, you will be able to manifest your intentions much faster. This is because now you're no longer bothered about the outcome. The outcome that comes is met with acceptance, instead of trying to force an outcome. This small change in outlook makes you very mature as a healer.

You will also notice that the Reiki will become more effective – for now you're playing the game to your best ability without bothering about the way things should go. Live your life with detachment and make it a mystery that gradually unfolds.

How it works

When your mind holds too rigid a position, a thought becomes more difficult to manifest. Every time you say, "This should specifically happen", you're also ruling out the possibility of many other events happening. The mind at times might just picture something in the "this should not happen" category, and you attract it to you.

I am in no way trying to say that the balance between intention and desire is easy to achieve. It is in fact really difficult. However, after many attempts you'll finally strike gold. And rather than how it works, all I can say is, IT WORKS!

Exercises

1. On your detachment day, learn to accept people and situations as they are. The universe is at this moment perfectly the way it should be – to struggle against this moment is to struggle against the entire universe. Instead, accept and be detached from what people should be.

2. Whenever there is a problem, don't force solutions – let the solutions emerge spontaneously and you'll realise that the best solutions are thrown up.

3. Learn to live in the wisdom of uncertainty – when things are not certain, don't be insecure – know that life will throw up the most exciting challenges, events and people for you.

4. Finally, the *Gita* gives a very important direction when Krishna tells Arjuna that he must focus on the task at hand and not on the final result. Try your best and leave the rest to God. This does not mean being absolutely unbothered about your intention. Keeping it in mind will give you the power to do your best in the present. But once you have given your best, the universe is the judge. And an impartial one, for that matter. You just have to wait for the result. And if you've given your best, you won't be disappointed.

EXPERIENCE JOURNAL

Tool Name:

_____

Possible situations where you can apply it:

_____

_____

_____

_____

My experiences with the Power Tool:

Date	Situation	Experience

Improvements that need to be made in my approach:

_____

_____

_____

_____

Concluding Attitude Tools

The Attitude Tools section ends here. At this juncture, let me tell you that the most important tool you have is your attitude. To be able to use a weapon, you must be qualified to do so. A layman can't fire a missile or launch a nuclear bomb.

Likewise, your qualification to use the rest of the power tools that follow is to be able to grasp and attain the attitudes that have been outlined. If you can do that, you'll see that not only your Reiki power but also the effectiveness of the tools will increase. On the other hand, if you can't adopt these tools, the remaining power tools, though effective, will not realise their full potential.

MEDITATION TOOLS

6. Basic Relaxation
7. White Light Meditation
8. Glass Bottle Meditation
9. The Heart Process
10. Centring

MEDITATION TOOLS

The mind is the medium through which we all operate. And like a restless child or a monkey, the mind jumps from place to place. That's the basic tendency of the mind. But true greatness lies in achieving a situation where your mind is under your control. If that happens, you have at your disposal the services of the most powerful computer in the world.

A computer matching the capabilities of the human mind has never been built. But if it is ever built, then conservative estimates say that it shall fit into a 33-storeyed building! There are two reasons for using meditation – the first and long-term one, of course, is to calm the mind. But for a more short-term result, meditation captures the fancy of your mind and uses energy in the right direction.

To master meditation is to master yourself. Time and again, the greatest of spiritual masters have attributed their success to their habit of meditation. We also must meditate. But what should one meditate on? This section answers just that – and the wide range of meditations have been given not to confuse you, but to help choose a form of meditation that best suits each one of us.

Initially, meditation will be difficult – you may feel the urge to move your body, various irritations, itching and a desire to scream! While meditating, all these have been experienced by our participants. It may happen to you too. All of a sudden you may just open your eyes. But don't let these setbacks bother you. Sustained and regular practice will give you results that one can only dream of!

$$\boxed{6}$$

Basic Relaxation

What is it?

Before you begin to meditate, the agitated mind must be calmed. The basic relaxation exercise was not originally intended to be a power tool. But surprisingly, we realised that every meditation of ours made a start with the module that we choose to call 'Basic Relaxation'.

The reason is obvious: you need to relax before you can meditate powerfully. Many of you have done this in a way through Yoga – for instance, *shavasan* and *yoga nidra*. Still others may have done something via the Silva Method. This is the best way, however, developed and perfected after many trials and errors.

Obviously, this doesn't mean that this relaxation is customised for you. Each one of us being so unique, all have a different way to relax. So what is suggested is that you try out the exercise and adapt it to your needs. You must develop your own customised way to relax.

Prerequisites

❑ A dark room where you shall not be disturbed (preferable but not a must).

❑ Comfortable place to lie down (don't lie down on the ground, but on a mattress).

❑ Loose clothes.

❑ Remove any tight belts/leather articles you may have.

❑ Drink some water before and after you start.

❑ Do not do this immediately after lunch/dinner unless you wish to sleep!

❑ If you can't remember this process, have someone to guide you through it. The other option would be to record all this in your voice and play it.

❑ All throughout this process it is very important to keep your eyes closed. The entire effect will be lost the moment you open your eyes.

❑ Also make sure that your body does not move at all. This will ensure perfect relaxation.

❑ It is best if you have not done any such activity that provokes thoughts before this – something like a heated discussion or even watching a violent movie on TV.

The actual process

Lie down on the mattress.

Gaze at the ceiling for some time (the blank portion). Try not to blink – close your eyes gradually, as they get moist.

Now for the next few minutes, let your attention be focused on your breathing.

Start deep abdominal breathing. This means that with every inhalation, your stomach should go up, and with exhalation it should come down. Keep your attention on your breathing.

As you start doing this, you will feel more and more relaxed.

Now one by one you will bring your attention to different parts of the body.

First focus attention on your hair... feel them relax. Then move your attention to the head, brain and forehead. Let them relax. Move your attention to your eyes and let them relax. Go on to your ears... your nose and lips... your cheeks and chin.

Your entire head is now relaxed.

If there is tension in any part of your body, mentally request it to relax. Now take your attention to your neck. Let it relax. Shift your attention down to the chest and lungs. Feel them getting more and more relaxed. Focus attention on your shoulders. Relax them completely.

Shift your attention to the left hand... left arm, elbow, wrist and the palm. Feel them getting more and more relaxed.

Do the same with your right hand, feel it being relaxed too.

Move attention back to your stomach – your liver, pancreas, intestines... feel the relaxation seep deep into your body. Take your attention to the back, lower back. Feel them getting more and more relaxed.

Turn your attention to the lower abdomen – your navel, genitals and buttocks. Let them relax.

Now take your attention to the left leg – the thighs, knee, calf, ankle and foot. Let each of these parts relax.

Similarly, turn your attention to the right leg – the thighs, knee, calf, ankle and foot. The relaxation spreads to this foot too.

Now your entire body is relaxed. You are absolutely still and calm. You will notice that the stillness in your body is accompanied by relaxation in your mind too. This will make a big difference to the level of relaxation.

Now start counting down from 99 to 10... with every number that you speak, you will get more and more relaxed. You will go deeper and deeper into relaxation with every number that is counted downwards. Count very slowly, making sure you relax each time you do this.

Once you reach ten, visualise each number from 9 to 1. Put in any bright colour that you want. After counting down to one, you shall be even more relaxed. To improve this further, go even deeper into relaxation by repeating the word "relax" with each breath.

Remember that all this time your breathing is deep. At this stage you shall be totally relaxed. Be in this state for some time.

Coming out of relaxation

Mentally tell yourself that you will now come out of the relaxation session feeling much better.

Now count up from 1 to 3.

Gradually begin to get movement in your body – the fingers and hands, and get a feel of the environment. Become aware of your surroundings.

Now slowly turn to your left. Lie down for some time.

As you get up, slowly sit up and gradually open your eyes. You will feel fresher. Don't jump into instant activity.

Effects and changes

With relaxation, you are ready to begin any meditation. You will see Basic Relaxation as a prerequisite for meditation. This is because it calms the mind and makes it much more receptive to ideas that are being fed in.

You will notice that when you're relaxed your thought process is very clear. You can also get lots of creative ideas when relaxed. This is the best time to talk to loved ones, clarify tough problems and make decisions. When relaxed, the body's healing process acts faster. This is because your subconscious mind makes it possible. Similarly, giving Reiki also becomes more effective after relaxation.

In the long run, being relaxed keeps you stress free and increases your lifespan. That's one of the best reasons to practise this daily – it increases your lifespan.

How it works

The entire principle of relaxation is that your subconscious mind is much more powerful than the conscious one. When you relax, the subconscious takes over.

To cite a metaphor, your subconscious is like the staff that works on the lower floors of the office building. The conscious mind is the CEO on the top floor. Even though it appears that the CEO is all-powerful, it is not so. The CEO cannot do anything without the support of the staff.

So the whole idea is to get to the level of the staff and make it cooperate. When you relax, communication directly happens with your subconscious. All through the day, your conscious mind jealously guards the subconscious mind. This is because the subconscious has no thinking power of its own. It is like a mad robot that will follow the instructions you give it.

All day, the conscious mind plays the role of the sentry, allowing very little information to percolate to the subconscious. But when you relax the conscious mind, you can see the difference. And what a difference it is!

Exercises

There are no specific exercises for Basic Relaxation. However, it is suggested that you try it whenever you have time – travelling, waiting for someone, when you're ill. You'll see improved health.

The shortcut to instant relaxation is deep breathing. Do deep breathing for five minutes any time in the day to make a big difference to your energy levels.

EXPERIENCE JOURNAL

Tool Name:

_____

Possible situations where you can apply it:

_____

_____

_____

My experiences with the Power Tool:

Date	Situation	Experience

Improvements that need to be made in my approach:

_____

_____

_____

7

White Light Meditation

What is it?

Mystics who have visualised Reiki energy have seen it as white or golden light. Even when Master Mikao Usui was meditating in an attempt to discover Reiki, he was struck with a brilliant light that was golden or white in colour. The white light meditation is a process where you combine the twin powers of Reiki and visualisation to produce the most dramatic effects.

In Reiki introduction talks, we teach white light. The benefit of white light is that *it can be done even by people who have not been attuned to channel Reiki.* However, Reiki channels will obviously be able to get better results. Still, we have found white light to be a great tool in convincing people to do Reiki.

The best thing about this meditation is the fact that it can be applied to events beyond space and time. If you have not done the second degree of Reiki, you can still transmit distant Reiki with the help of white light.

One of our participants had to leave the workshop before he could be attuned. However, he learnt the white light meditation. Two years down the line we happened to meet him – and we were pleasantly surprised by the kind of results he was producing! It was in fact much better than many of our Reiki participants. This is the power of white light.

Prerequisites

❑ A dark room where you shall not be disturbed (preferable but not a must).

❑ Comfortable place to sit down (don't lie down on the ground or mattress; you may sit on a chair).

❑ Loose clothes.

❑ Remove any tight belts/leather articles you may have.

❑ Drink some water before and after you start.

❑ It is strongly recommended that someone guide you through the process.

❑ Throughout this process it is very important to keep your eyes closed. The entire effect will be lost the moment you open your eyes.

❑ This meditation can also be done in a group.

❑ If you're doing white light in a group, form a white light circle. Sit in a circle and let each person cup hands. Put your right hand on top of the hand of the person to the right of you and the left under the person to the left. In this way, each person shall have one of his hands up and the other down.

❑ The hand that is up is for giving while the hand that is down (the left) is for receiving energy.

The actual process

Start with the basic relaxation process. Proceed further only after you have entered a state of deep relaxation. Till then, keep chanting the word "relax" with each breath you inhale and exhale.

Now slowly visualise a ball of brilliant white light over your crown chakra, about one foot in the area over your head. The ball is one of brilliant white light, sparkling with radiance. It is pure energy that is about to enter your body.

Once the image of the ball is visualised, feel the energy coming into your body through your crown chakra. The brilliant white light enters and fills your head, neck, upper body, hands, lower abdomen and finally your feet.

Your entire body is now filled with brilliant white light. The white light is liquid and free flowing. It is washing away all your negativity. Your body is now entirely cleansed by this white light. Feel the white light energy flowing in your body, circulating at a rapid pace.

Now take your attention to your heart chakra. Imagine the white light is concentrated on your heart chakra, just the way Reiki flows through it.

From your heart, it is flowing to your right hand. You are giving energy to the person sitting on your right. However, the vacuum that is created by this is filled up with more and more white light from the infinite ball above your head. Imagine the white light flowing to the person on the right and connecting to the white light in his or her body.

At the same time, take your focus to the left hand, where you are receiving energy. Feel the energy coming to you and be open to receive it.

Now your entire group has formed what is called the White Light Circle. Brilliant white light is flowing from your body. You have formed a group of people who are sharing white light.

Now expand this white light of your group to fill up the entire room you're in. The entire room is now covered with white light.

Expand it further to the building. Feel the flow of white light energy to every home in the vicinity, to the entire building. Expand the circle further to make it cover the entire locality that you are in. Feel the people receiving energy from your white light circle.

Further, expand it to cover the entire city. Move on to the state and, finally, let the white light cover the entire country. Your white light circle is spreading happiness and joy in the entire country. Visualise all the people of your nation as happy, prosperous and satisfied.

Take the circle to expand it to the whole world – cover all the continents and now visualise the entire planet to be filled with white light. Let there be an experience of peace all around the world.

Expand the white light further to cover the entire universe – the solar system, all the stars and the Milky Way, and finally the other galaxies. Spread the white light everywhere – don't leave any spot untouched.

At this stage, you can take the meditation to any direction that you want. Here are a few options:

General white light

Visualise your favourite place in detail. Experience how you feel out there. Feel the joy within you. Acknowledge it. And cover this place with white light.

Now visualise yourself with your favourite person at this place. This makes you feel very happy and relaxed. Cover both yourself and the person with white light.

Add a small prayer for the well-being of yourself and the other person.

For an intention

Hold the intention in your mind – imagine as if the intention is already fulfilled. How would you feel then? Would you be happy? Rejoicing? Celebrating? Feel the joy. Cover this scene with white light.

Pray for detachment from the outcome and for strength in your efforts.

For a situation

Visualise not the current situation, but the way you want it to be. After you do this in detail, i.e., adding colour, sounds and movement to it, you must cover the scene with white light.

Pray for an outcome that is best for most people.

For a person

Visualise the person as perfectly healthy and glowing. Send the person white light and see him getting covered with white light. Feel him getting healed and cured.

Pray for his well-being.

Past event

For healing a past event, it is recommended that you use the forgiveness meditation.

Effects and changes

Initial practice of white light may become very challenging since you're not used to visualisation, but soon it shall become lucid. As I have mentioned many times in the book, if this tool is used in conjunction with other tools, the effect will be much better.

So give white light to an intention and see it manifest. Don't forget the detachment!

People have used white light in the most challenging circumstances. You can recover lost things, bring about healings and empower your greater intentions using white light.

How it works

When the seven colours of the spectrum merge, they form the colour white. Hence, white by its very nature is a very holistic colour. This divine light is related to spiritual energy – white light is also referred to as *Divya Prakash.*

Also, anything is always created twice – first in the mind and then in reality. This is true for whatever you want. When you use white light, you are already holding a picture in your mind. And you will attract what you hold in your mind.

Exercises

With white light, there is no limit to the number of uses you can put it to. Giving exercises would mean restricting its scope; so our message for this one is – just play around with it. Wherever you see the need, start the white light. From a crying baby to some national problem, your imagination is the limit.

EXPERIENCE JOURNAL

Tool Name:

_____

Possible situations where you can apply it:

_____

_____

My experiences with the Power Tool:

Date	Situation	Experience

Improvements that need to be made in my approach:

_____

_____

_____

8

Glass Bottle Meditation

"To give, we must have in plenty ourselves."
—Swami Chinmayananda

What is it?

Glass bottle meditation is one of the quickest ways to relax and de-stress your body. Even if you're a Reiki channel, stress is capable of reducing the flow of energy within you. When you do not have enough for yourself, whenever you channel Reiki for others too, it shall first fill up your needs and thus not be so effective.

The glass bottle meditation is a simple tool to get fresh instantly. The first time I was exposed to it, the sceptic in me emerged – why not white light? Isn't that good enough? The answer is that it is. But glass bottle is a better option to release stress. It is like the difference between a general physician and a specialist. Your white light is nothing but a general physician that can cure any and many disorders – on the other hand, glass bottle is like a specialist for stress relief. Sure enough, once I tried it, I realised how true it was!

Prerequisites

❑ A dark room where you shall not be disturbed (preferable but not a must).

❑ Comfortable place to sit down (you may lie down on the ground, or you may sit on a chair).

❑ Loose clothes.

❏ Remove any tight belts/leather articles you may have.

❏ Drink some water before and after you start.

❏ There is no need for a guide in this process; it can be done easily on your own.

❏ Throughout this process it is very important to keep your eyes closed. The entire effect will be lost the moment you open your eyes.

❏ This meditation is to be done solo.

❏ Connection with the earth is very vital – direct connection. So ensure that even when you're sitting on a chair, your feet touch the ground. Make sure you're barefoot.

The actual process

Do the basic relaxation process first.

Once you're completely relaxed, focus on your breathing for some time.

Now imagine your body to be a glass bottle – your head and neck form the upper part of the bottle and the rest of your body is the body of the bottle.

Feel contained in the shape of the bottle – you are in the glass bottle now.

Now visualise the bottle filled with a dark brown and heavy liquid. This is in every part of your body – it represents all the stress, heaviness and negativity that you have accumulated during the day.

Feel the heaviness for some time.

Now slowly feel the ends of your limbs – hands and feet – to be taps. Open these taps. The dark brown liquid slowly starts to drain out from the limbs.

As it drains, you feel more and more light.

It has slowly drained from the head and then your upper torso, escaping from the finger taps [sic] of your hand.

The liquid of the lower abdomen and legs drains from the tap of the toes.

Gradually, all your body is hollow and empty.

You are now filling your body with energy.

Let liquid white light fill your body.

Feel the energy – and relax.

Effects and changes

Glass bottle acts as an instant stress reliever.

I remember the first time I was made to do this process. The sceptic within me emerged and said it did not make any sense to use this – white light was much better. But I decided to go through with an open mind. And indeed, focused meditation helps the cause better. Call glass bottle a remixed visualisation. Or call it a variation of white light. The bottom line is – it works.

Do this daily at the end of the day to relax. Even after you return from work, you will feel the energy to go on and on and on.

How it works

Glass bottle is a focused version of creative visualisation – when you use glass bottle meditation, you are doing nothing but a specific visualisation.

The first step that you take is to recognise the existence of stress, grant it a sense of legitimacy by visualising the heavy dark brown liquid. This helps you know and feel the nagging feeling of stress – by specifically pinpointing it, you can eliminate it faster.

The next part involves feelings with visualisation. FEELINGS. That's the key word here. You can actually feel the stress go out, along with the tension and pressures. This corresponds to the visualisation, making each other more and more powerful.

Finally, the idea of actually making the liquid go from taps makes more sense than just imagining the liquid evaporating.

Exercises

Use variants of glass bottle meditation. Instead of the white light, you can fill up the light of any colour you desire for corresponding effect. Proponents of colour therapy have a great chance to use colour here. Others can, however, just use white or golden light.

EXPERIENCE JOURNAL

Tool Name:

_____

Possible situations where you can apply it:

_____

_____

_____

My experiences with the Power Tool:

Date	Situation	Experience

Improvements that need to be made in my approach:

_____

_____

_____

9

The Heart Process

What is it?

"Don't break my heart!" Isn't this an oft-repeated phrase amongst most youngsters? Do you know why? Because hearts are where your emotions are. We have all heard references to the heart in thousands of Bollywood songs – in fact across cultures, the heart represents love and emotions.

Emotions, as experts reveal, are 17 times more powerful than rational thought. In all the other meditations that you have done and practised so far, you have been using your mind – the rational thought. But in the heart process, you switch to using emotions and instinct, which is far more powerful than the most powerful thoughts that you have ever had.

While thoughts just affect the brain, emotions alter your physiology. You may have thoughts of happiness, but that will be useless, unless you actually feel happy. Most of us are yet to reach a level where the thought becomes so powerful that it alters not only the physiology but also the mental make-up. For the rest of us, there are emotions. Think of the time when you're really happy – you feel a sense of warmth and expansive love. There is a sense of connection with your surroundings. The body posture is relaxed – you are comfortable and smiling. That's the effect of emotions. Biologically too, when you're happy, a number of hormones and chemicals are released that make you feel really good.

Another example I often cite in my workshops is of a person crossing the street. Imagine you're crossing a busy road and you absentmindedly fail to look to one side of the road. Suddenly, you hear honking from that very side. It is a speeding vehicle and instinctively the body steps back. Now, did you have a thought that went: "This is a car. I have to be safe. This can ram into me. So I will step back. I must step back now..." No! Your instinct was what pushed you. That's what the power of instinctive emotions is all about.

So what we are now going to do is access the most intuitive and wonderful gifts that have been bestowed upon you, in the Heart Process.

Prerequisites

- ❏ A dark room where you shall not be disturbed (preferable but not a must).
- ❏ Soft music is recommended.
- ❏ Comfortable place to sit down (you may sit on a chair).
- ❏ Loose clothes.
- ❏ Remove any tight belts/leather articles you may have.
- ❏ Drink some water before and after you start.
- ❏ For this process, it is recommended that somebody guide you.
- ❏ Throughout, it is very important to keep your eyes closed. The entire effect will be lost the moment you open your eyes.
- ❏ This meditation is to be done solo.

The actual process

Do the basic relaxation process first.

Once you're completely relaxed, focus on your breathing for some time.

Now take a long deep breath and put your right hand slowly on your heart.

Slowly put your left hand on your *hara* (the sixth chakra on the energy column, responsible for the creative instinct and sexual desire), which lies just below the navel.

Imagine you're being filled to the brim with love.

There is love both outside and inside you.

Gradually take your attention to the heart.

Feel it being filled with the golden white light of love.

You are slowly getting more and more relaxed.

Now imagine this golden light centre in a sort of ball in your heart.

From your heart this energy is slowly expanding to touch every part of your body.

Start with your head – let the love energy touch it. Mentally express love to every part – your hair, brain, forehead, eyes, eyebrows, nose, cheeks, lips, teeth, mouth, ears and chin.

Come down to your neck, the food pipe and windpipe – cover them all with love. Come down to your shoulders and upper back. Send love energy to your lungs and to the heart itself, which is the centre of all love.

Take it to each of the hands and to your stomach, pancreas and liver. Spread the love to your lower abdomen. Take it to your genitals. Then to each leg.

Now your entire body is covered in love. It is like being in the lap of your mother – never before have you experienced such deep, intense love.

Now turn your attention to the heart. The heart has always been there for you – beating ceaselessly, pumping blood and providing you with energy and vitality. From the first breath to your last, the heart has been with you throughout.

Unlike what most of you believe, the heart is not emotional and thereby irrational. However, it is holistic, being connected to the cosmic computer. It can sense what most of our senses and rational thoughts miss.

Thank this heart for serving you tirelessly all the while. Express your gratitude to this wonderful organ, which many believe is the seat of the mind.

The responses from the heart are never in words – they are in feelings. A feeling of comfort is a positive response. Discomfort is negative. It's more the way your heart makes you feel. Learning to recognise this is very important for going beyond this process.

The first question to ask your heart is whether it is willing to talk to you. Wait till it agrees. If you feel the response is that of discomfort, repeat the request a few times. The heart loves you and will agree.

However, if you're not comfortable with it, the heart will give you a negative response. If that is the case, do not force the heart. Let go. Express gratitude and end the process. Lie down for some time and relax.

Most times your heart will want to talk to you.

Ask your heart if you really love yourself. So many of us have never taken time to actually love ourselves. Maybe it is the conditioning that we received in our childhood. It might even have something to do with your values. But you need to realise that loving yourself is of utmost importance.

Know the response and this will give you some realisation about yourself.

Next, ask whether you take enough care of yourself. Many of us tend to ignore our priorities for those of others. Some of us do it out of sheer laziness. Either way, it doesn't make any sense to ignore yourself. Treat your body as the temple of God.

Ask your heart if you are physically and mentally fit – are you really living at the level where you want to be? Do you deserve more?

Then ask yourself whether you take care of yourself. And your likes and dislikes? Many of us fail to pay attention to even this seemingly unimportant thing.

Remember that you need to take enough time to ask the question and let your heart respond. The heart's behaviour is definitely not rational – by our standards it is more eccentric. But the heart never lies. It will never tell you something that is either harmful for you or something that is disempowering.

Once you have done this, you can express gratitude to your heart and slowly come out of the process.

Lie down or wait for some time.

Effects and changes

The heart process makes you love unconditionally. For any relationship, a part of unconditional love is also important. So with the heart process you will learn to love unconditionally.

Listening to your heart also means not holding back what you really feel. At the Thakore Centre, we have done research on this and the evidence says it all. Men have many more heart attacks than women and they are almost twice as likely to suffer it.

We all know that men take time to express what they feel, while women can not only express but also cry at something unpleasant. This emotional release relieves the heart. And that is really good for the heart.

While doing this process, many people realise that all their lives they had been busy living for others. They never got any time to take care of themselves. This is the case particularly with many housewives.

We have also observed that older people above 40 find this process more enjoyable. This is because once everything is settled, they can actually realise this. Maybe this is also the right time to actually receive the insight!

Beyond 40 you tend to get more time for yourself and often do not know what to do with that time. This is when the heart process can be a major eye-opener.

After this process, many actually realise that they have been ignoring their hobbies and passions – this process will make you realise that you should enjoy life NOW and not wait for something to happen.

How it works

The heart is the centre of love. When you tune in to the heart, you are attuned to the cosmic computer. The driving force behind this tool is the power of love.

To understand it better, I quote from my book *31 Days to a New You*, on the Power of Love:

Just for Today I Will Spread the Love.

It's love that makes the world go round!

The most noble of emotions that man experiences is love – when you love, you can truly be your higher self. Love also brings out the best in others. Look at a mother who loves her child, or a lover who longs for his beloved. Love is universal, but what I suggest is that it must become a universal currency!

One of my gurus is Sri Sri Ravishankar, who is actually an embodiment of such divine love, one look at his photograph will make you smile. His presence will make you feel the warmth within – this is one man who radiates love. Similar experiences have been reported to me on seeing other spiritual gurus like Satya Sai Baba, Asaram Bapu and Osho Rajneesh. This is simply because these people have learnt to spread love.

If you've experienced love, you'll know how pure it makes you. The feeling is that of perfection and invincibility. It is complete bliss and joy; indeed such is the power of love!

If that's the magic of love, it's something very odd,
For it makes you feel that someone is almost like God!

However, what you must have been experiencing up to now is selective love – meant only for your loved ones, relatives and friends. What I suggest is something more and different from this – it is to love universally. It is to love everyone without any prejudice or preconceived notions. Just love for the sake of it, for love that you have inherent within you for your fellow beings.

Such love is also unconditional. If you look at love these days, it has become more of a commercial deal. If you do this, I'll love you and if you do that, I will not! It's subject to conditions – and more of a power struggle. That's how the so-called magic of love fades and relationships get soured.

When a disciple asked the master how he could get that magic back into his love, the master said, "Ask as a favour what you had been claiming as a right up to now!" How true! That's the small difference that makes a big difference. Love is all about unconditional acceptance rather than changing people.

Universal love means love for all. Just for today, fill yourself with love and project that love to all. Talk to everyone lovingly and forgive his or her mistakes. Just like a mother, who may scold a child momentarily, but will never ever want to harm the child. That's the kind of love you need.

You will know you have it when others see a perennial twinkle in your eyes and a smile on your face. When others feel extremely comfortable in your company. It's nothing that can be taught – but yes, it is always possible to experience it.

Hugging is something we are so hesitant to do – but it's a beautiful way of expressing love. Most of us don't even get one hug per day. We need at least three for well-being, while the ideal is 12! So start a hugging war – hug each other whenever you meet.

True love will fill every moment of your existence with vibrancy and wonder. That's the magic of love!

Exercises

1. Just for today, feel yourself filled with love, like a balloon.

2. Whenever you meet someone, mentally project love to him or her.

3. Hug your loved ones – you need a minimum of three hugs per day!

4. Just for today, don't try to change people – love them unconditionally.

Specifically for Power Tools

1. Whenever you have to take a decision, spare a moment to consult your heart. Do this by centring yourself first and turn your attention towards the heart. Ask your heart what to do as you do in the heart process.

2. After you have done this, don't stop. When you pursue a particular course of action, check your feelings about it. If you don't feel right, do not do it, come what may.

3. You can use the heart process to answer questions too – once you've asked the initial questions, you can put the

most complex questions to your heart. You'll be surprised at the kind of results and answers it produces. Remember to be detached though!

4. Healing a past event through the heart process is also a wonderful experience. Recollect the person and the experience and mentally forgive the person. Ask your heart to send love to the person.

Do not forget, LOVE IS POWER!

EXPERIENCE JOURNAL

Tool Name:

_____

Possible situations where you can apply it:

_____

_____

_____

My experiences with the Power Tool:

Date	Situation	Experience

Improvements that need to be made in my approach:

_____

_____

_____

10

Centring

What is it?

Most Reiki practitioners know the chakra system. Chakras are basically energy centres – places in the body where the life force energy tends to centre around. There are seven main chakras located along your spinal chord; each has its own functions, colours and properties. The energy thus tends to travel along this column, from top to bottom as in the case of Reiki or from bottom to top as in the case of Kundalini.

The knowledge of chakras is essential to the person who is guiding you through this meditation. After doing it a few times, you too shall become familiar with the whole process. After all it is the language of your body, your soul!

Prerequisites

You need basic knowledge about the chakra system. There are many books available on the topic and you can pick any of them for ready information. Here is a small ready reference:

Chakras

Chakra is a Sanskrit word for "wheel". Chakras are described as being shaped like multicoloured lotus petals or spoked wheels, which whirl at different speeds as they process energy. They are described in Hindu and Buddhist yogic literature. Both systems describe them differently and their descriptions vary in Western literature as well.

Scientifically, chakras are not recognised, as no evidence of them exists. It is only recently that they have not completely been dismissed by Western medicine. Their increased acknowledgment has come about from the use of acupuncture meridians and other Eastern systems in healing the body. Although controversial, evidence about the existence of chakras was presented by Hiroshi Motoyama of Japan. He hypothesised that if an enlightened individual could influence the chakras, the energy output would be measured. Using a lead-lined recording booth, Motoyama measured the energy field opposite various chakras, which subjects claimed to have awakened, usually through years of meditation. His findings were that energy levels at those areas were significantly greater than over the same areas of a controlled subject.

The methods of diagnosing the health of chakras are by clairvoyance, energy scans with the hands, and dowsing with pendulums. Clairvoyants say that health disturbances often manifest in the aura, and thus in the chakras, months and sometimes years before they appear in the physical body.

There are seven major chakras and hundreds of minor ones. In the aura, the etheric, astral and mental bodies are said to have seven major chakras each. The seven major etheric centres, which are most directly concerned with physical health, lie along the spinal column. Each is associated with an endocrine gland, a major nerve plexus, a physiological function and a psychic function. The higher the position along the spinal column, the more complex is the chakra and the higher are its functions.

The chakras are connected to one another and the body through *nadis*, channels of subtle energy. Of the thousands of nadis, three are most important. The *sushumna*, the central channel, originating at the base of the spine and rising to the medulla oblongata at the base of the brain; it processes energy coming from the etheric field. The *ida* and *pingala* likewise extend from the base of the spine to the brow and end at the left and right nostrils. They criss-cross the *sushumna* in a spiral that resembles the caduceus. They wrap around, but do not penetrate the chakras, and manage the outflow of energy.

The universal life force, or *kundalini*, is said to enter the aura through the chakra via the top of the head and is filtered down to the other chakras, each of which transforms the energy into the precise usable form of energy for the function it controls. When this universal force is aroused, it rises up the chakra system through the *sushumna*.

When the person is in good health, each chakra clearly shows its own colouration and the number of petal spokes and has an even speed of vibration. In poor health, their colouration becomes cloudy and the rotation irregular and sluggish.

The seven basic etheric chakras are the root, the sacral, the solar plexus, the heart, the throat, the brow and the crown.

1. **The root** (*muladhara*) is located at the base of the spine and is the seat of the *kundalini*. It is concerned with self-preservation, one's animal nature, taste and smell. It is the least complex of all the chakras and is just divided by four spokes. Its colour is orange-red.

2. **The sacral** (*svadhisthana*) lies near the genitals and governs sexuality and reproduction. It has six spokes and is primary red. In some systems the root chakra is ascribed reproductive functions, and the sacral chakra is overlooked in favour of the spleen chakra, a rosy pink and yellow sun with six spokes located halfway between the pubis and the navel. It influences general health and particularly governs digestion and the functions of the liver, pancreas and spleen. In other systems, the spleen chakra is seen as minor.

3. **The solar plexus** (*manipurna*) rests just above the navel. It has ten spokes and is predominantly green and light red. It is associated with emotions and is the point where astral energy enters the etheric field. This chakra affects the adrenals, pancreas, liver and stomach. Most trance mediums work through the solar plexus.

4. **The heart** (*anahata*) has 12 glowing golden petals and is located midway between the shoulder blades, in the middle of the chest. It governs the thymus gland and influences immunity to disease. It is linked to higher consciousness and unconditional love.

5. **The throat** (*visuddha*) is a 16-spoke wheel of silvery blue colour that is associated with creativity, self-expression and the search for Truth. It is predominant in musicians, singers, composers and public speakers. This chakra influences the thyroid and parathyroid glands, metabolism, and is associated with certain states of expanded consciousness.

6. **The brow** (*ajna*) is located between the eyebrows and is sometimes called the third eye because of its influence over the psychic sense and spiritual enlightenment. Half of its 96 spokes are radiated in a yellow-rose colour, while the other half are radiated in blue and purple. The chakra is associated with the pituitary and pineal glands, intelligence, intuition and psychic powers called *siddhis* in yoga.

7. **The crown** (*sahasrara*) whirls above the top of the head. Its 972 spokes radiate a glowing purple, the most spiritual of all the colours. It is not associated with any gland, but reveals the person's conscious evolution. The crown cannot be activated until all the other chakras are refined and balanced; when activated it brings supreme enlightenment and cosmic consciousness. While other chakras rotate in slight depressions, the crown chakra whirls in a dome. At times, in religious art, crown chakras have been portrayed as halos surrounding the heads of deities, saints and mystics.

Go through this information till you familiarise yourself with the chakra system thoroughly.

The other prerequisites are more or less the same:

❑ A dark room where you shall not be disturbed (preferable but not a must).

❑ Comfortable place to sit down (you may sit in a chair but do not lie down). Connection with the ground is advisable.

❑ Loose clothes.

❑ Remove any tight belts/leather articles you may have.

❑ Drink some water before and after you start.

❑ For this process, it is recommended that somebody guide you.

❑ Throughout, it is very important to keep your eyes closed. The entire effect will be lost the moment you open your eyes.

The actual process

First do the basic relaxation.

Now visualise a fist-sized ball at the top of your crown chakra.

Let the image be there and solidify it.

We shall guide this through your chakra system.

This golden ball of energy now enters your body through the crown chakra.

Let it stay stable on the crown chakra as you feel the energy going into the chakra.

The thousand-petal chakra will absorb energy. Visualise its violet colour. Let the ball turn violet too.

After some time, take a long deep breath. Hold for some time. With a quick exhalation bring the ball down to the third eye chakra. Visualise the colour purple/indigo as you turn your attention between the eyebrows. The ball becomes that colour too.

Experience the qualities of the crown chakra – alertness and a sense of intuition.

When you feel complete with this, take a long breath, hold it for some time and exhale quickly. Along with the exhalation, the ball now moves to your throat chakra. Imagine the colour blue here. Feel the ball of energy turning blue to send the energy across.

Feel your communication getting clearer as your chakra absorbs the energy.

Now take a deep breath. With a very quick exhalation let the ball reach your heart chakra. The colour for visualisation and the ball is green. Feel the love in your life expanding as your chakra absorbs more and more energy. Relax.

After the heart, another deep breath will take you to the solar plexus. Let the ball now assume a different colour – yellow. Let energy connect to the emotions stored here.

Take another deep breath to take your ball of golden light further down the column. Now as you exhale quickly, the ball reaches your *hara* or navel chakra. The colour has turned orange. Feel the energy at your *hara* as your unexpressed emotions are released and creativity blooms.

With a deep breath exhale and take the ball to the base of your spine. It should almost seem as if you are sitting on the ball. This is your base chakra. Visualise the colour red and let energy nourish your basic survival instincts.

Now turn your attention to the entire spine at one go.

Let your hands clasp, with thumbs pointing towards the sky, as you breathe deeply.

Feel energy all over your spine as the ball dissolves into pure energy flowing all over the column.

Let the energy get more and more intense. Visualise it getting more and more effective.

Finally, let the energy from the column gradually seep into your body. With a balance of energy at your chakras, you shall feel much better.

Be in the energetic state for some time.

Finally, when you feel all right, slowly open your eyes.

Effects and changes

You will observe that each one of us has problems at different chakras. When you think of it, every disease has a psychological cause and stems from imbalance in energy at one of the centres.

On doing this exercise, many experience emotions that they never felt before. This is because when you focus on a particular chakra, you are consciously inviting the related emotions to come forth and manifest.

The energy experienced in this meditation is very different from white light, because you keep adding each component of energy to separate chakras. This meditation is like a prism, which breaks up the white light meditation into specific energies for each of the chakras.

How it works

For the seeker, the chakra system is an unquestioned and an unquestionable reality. Responding to this, the meditation mainly helps you balance the energy in all the different chakras.

Any disorder stemming out of imbalance in a particular chakra will be nullified by this meditation.

The prime reason for it working is the fact that it channels the power of focus. When you concentrate on any particular area with total and undivided attention, you are trying to see it as whole.

Add colour to it and you will see that you are tuning to the level of the energy of that very chakra. Being aware of the associated emotions helps too.

Exercises

1. *Physical balancing of the chakras.* This is a technique we recommend you learn under a Reiki teacher. It involves the experiencing of energy of each chakra and then adjusting it with the corresponding one. Remember, the crown chakra never needs to be balanced.

2. *Chakra awareness.* At different points of time in the day, turn your attention to any particular chakra and send it love energy. Experience the renewed energy.

3. *Emotional awareness.* The next time you experience an emotion, say a surge of creativity or sudden love, try to see where the emotion is physically located. You will be surprised by the results!

4. *Meditation on the chakras.* One of the recommended meditations is to just sit in silence for some time and then turn your entire attention to a particular chakra and keep it there for some time.

EXPERIENCE JOURNAL

Tool Name:

_____

Possible situations where you can apply it:

_____

_____

_____

My experiences with the Power Tool:

Date	Situation	Experience

Improvements that need to be made in my approach:

_____

_____

_____

Concluding Meditation Tools

The whole idea of this section is that you experience the meditations. Mere reading is not even the remotest of substitutes for real practice. Get a partner or, better still, form a group so that you can assist each other through the meditations.

One of the more amusing things I have discovered in Reiki is that each one of us tends to develop his/her favourite meditation – the one that gives the most results and proves the most enjoyable. While there is nothing wrong about having a favourite, you are still advised to practise all the meditations in equal proportion, more so because they have a complementing effect on each other.

In the short term, there may be no visible benefits of the meditations. But in the long run, you will discover the tremendous transformation that these meditations can bring you.

One last word – the most important thing is to be flexible in your approach. The plan that works for you is the best plan. So feel free to modify these meditations till you are comfortable – as long as you do not change their essence. Play around and enjoy!

VERBAL TOOLS

VERBAL TOOLS

The word has power – a spoken word contains within itself thoughts, ideas and deep meaning and reveals the deepest recesses of your mind. In the verbal tools section, we will learn to tap the power of the word to actually empower our intentions and magnify our positivism.

Almost every culture, however ancient, has practices that involve chanting – prayers, mantras or hymns. The power of the word is so immense that verbal tools alone can alter your entire life. This happens, of course, when you begin to put it into practice and then notice the results.

The chapters from now on also become a little shorter, since no unwanted explanation is provided. Let the experience you have be the best proof of your success. So are you really raring to go? Let's unleash the magnificent power of words and create massive changes that you have never dreamt of. See the effect of words already?

11

Affirmations

What is it?

An affirmation basically is a positive statement of intention – it is set in the future, as if you have already got what you wanted.

How to use

Affirmations can be spoken or written.

A typical affirmation is spoken three times with full belief thrice a day – when you wake up, when you are about to sleep, and sometime during the middle part of the day.

Check the exercises for more details on how to use them for specific issues.

Effects and changes

Affirmations are one of the most powerful tools to transform you – once you begin to repeat these, you will notice that within a short while they become a part of your inner voice. One of the greatest choices we have in life is to create and choose our own reality and that's where affirmations come in.

You can affirm something simple and powerful all the time and notice the massive improvement in your life.

How it works

Your subconscious mind is like a field where you plant seeds of positive and negative thoughts. As you sow so shall you reap – that is the universal rule. But remember that you reap manifold. Over 90% of our thoughts are negative – and you can see that we manifest this in life.

Exercises

I've enjoyed using affirmations for several years. It is free, easy and usually effective. For myself, it is simply repeating a *positive* phrase before the mirror, in the car, or writing it on paper. Whenever I catch myself thinking something I don't wish to, I try to "change that thought" to a new one.

Here are some techniques I use with affirmations to change my behaviour. Feel free to modify them for your own use as I have for mine.

1. *Mirror technique.* This technique is great for helping you see yourself beautiful. I learned this from Louise Hay's books and modified it for my own use.

Stand before the mirror. Start at one end of your body and work to the other end finding as many nice things to say about your body as you can. For example: "I love my ears. They hear well and enable me to listen. They have a beautiful shape. I love my wonderful ears."

This technique helps you find and appreciate more of you. All the parts of your body perform important functions. Your eyes see, ears hear, nose smells and the heart pumps blood.

2. *Anywhere technique.* Whenever you catch yourself thinking something you would rather not, here is a technique that works rather well. It is based on NLP (neuro-linguistic programming).

Hear the phrase you said diminishing in volume until it disappears; then hear the phrase you wish to say grow louder. Alternately, you can see the "picture" of what you didn't like spin away from you and have the picture of what you want spin towards you.

3. *Writing technique.* I call this technique "Giving the problem to Spirit". Scott Adams used a version of this technique to change his life. It worked well for him; it can work for you too.

Simply sit down at a table and write what you would like in your life 15 times everyday. An example is: "I am healthy, happy, wise and free." When you are done, know that the universe is taking care of it.

4. *Trash-can technique.* Whenever you find something you don't like, write it down and throw it into the trash bin. By doing this, you are telling the universe, 'I want to be done with this problem. Please help me work through it and be done with it.'

Affirmations

❏ I feel loved every moment.

❏ I am healthy.

❏ I am happy.

❏ I take charge of my life.

- My eyes clearly see the world around me.
- I am wise.
- I am a spark of Divine Love.
- I am free.
- I listen to my spirit everyday.
- I am beautiful.
- I welcome new life to grow and be nurtured within me (for fertility).
- Divine Order takes charge of my life today and everyday.
- All things work for my good today.
- This is a new and wonderful day for me, there will never be another day like this one.
- I am divinely guided all day long and whatever I do will prosper.
- Divine Love surrounds me, enfolds me and enwraps me, and I go forth in peace.
- Whenever my attention wanders away from that which is good and constructive, I immediately bring it back to that which is lovely and good.
- I am a spiritual and mental magnet, attracting to myself all things that bless me.
- I am going to be a wonderful success in all my undertakings today.
- I am definitely going to be happy all day long.
- I am a brilliant and successful artist.
- I am allowed to nurture the artist within me.
- I am confident and competent in my creative work.
- I am tolerant of the ambiguity in problems.
- I am willing to be of service through my creativity.
- I am willing to create.
- I am willing to experience my creative energy.

- ❏ I am willing to learn to let myself create.
- ❏ I am willing to use my creative talents.
- ❏ I begin every task by thinking of new and better ways to accomplish it.
- ❏ I consider many possible solutions from diverse sources.
- ❏ I deserve a rewarding creative life.
- ❏ I have a constant flow of new and interesting ideas.
- ❏ I have an adventurous mind and see new experiences regularly.
- ❏ I have an unusual ability to reach creative decisions and to find creative solutions for problems.
- ❏ I have rich creative talents.
- ❏ I have the courage and self-confidence necessary to put my solutions into practice.
- ❏ I have the strength and persistence necessary to work ideas through to the solutions.
- ❏ I maintain a broad outlook towards life.
- ❏ I play with partial, incomplete and sometimes foolish ideas.
- ❏ I recognise the task of making mistakes but learn from them.
- ❏ I spend ten minutes each morning and evening thinking over problems.
- ❏ I treat each new problem I encounter as a new door to be opened and an opportunity to be creative.
- ❏ I trust my feelings and unconscious thoughts.
- ❏ My creativity always leads me to truth and love.
- ❏ My creativity heals others and myself.
- ❏ My creativity leads me to forgiveness and self-forgiveness.
- ❏ Through the use of a few simple tools, my creativity will flourish.

EXPERIENCE JOURNAL

Tool Name:

_____

Possible situations where you can apply it:

_____

_____

My experiences with the Power Tool:

Date	Situation	Experience

Improvements that need to be made in my approach:

_____

_____

_____

12

Jai Reiki and Cancel Cancel

What is it?

These are two power words that are akin to mantras. As soon as you evoke them, you will notice how powerful these can be. These are original techniques evolved by people who have made Reiki a way of life. These have been immensely effective for them.

How effective these words will be for you depends on how frequently you use them.

How to use

All you have to do is to mentally repeat these words as needed. When you say something in your mind, notice how you sound – how is your inner voice?

Check the feeling right now by telling yourself: "I love myself" or "I am great". How was the voice? Was it loud or soft? Was it coming from your heart or the whole body? Was it echoing or mono?

When you say something with total belief, your inner

voice sounds different. It is loud and comes from your heart. So when you say these two words, you will notice the positive changes these power words bring you.

Therefore, when you say "Jai Reiki", let it be loud and congruent – of course, in your inner voice and not as a slogan!

The same goes for 'cancel cancel', though that is expected to be more firm and strong.

When to use

Whenever you need a sudden dose of energy and have no time to relax, express gratitude or even centre yourself, use Jai Reiki.

For instance, you happen to be really scared of dogs and are one day confronted by a dog. The dog starts barking fiercely – what do you do? You need to take a deep breath, close your eyes and mentally say 'Jai Reiki'.

This is your call to the Reiki energy that you have so much faith in. Repeat the words thrice – for mind, body and spirit. When you say it, do this with faith and congruency. Pay particular attention to your inner voice and you will ensure that it sounds like the one you had wanted.

Regarding 'cancel cancel', you need to use it as soon as you say something negative or whatever you do NOT wish to. This is to correct you. Try to make it a habit to speak about what you want – what you want is more important. So don't say, "I don't want disease", say, "I want good health."

Now there will be times when you are considering the negative possibility. Say, "If this book is a failure..." as soon as I say that, I add "cancel cancel" to nullify the effect of what I just said.

Why this unnecessary formality? The reason is that as you progress on the path of Reiki you will realise that your words begin to have more and more power... you will be able to manifest all that you desire. Likewise, if you say something negative, it will come to pass. Hence 'cancel cancel'.

Effects and changes

Jai Reiki has a positive effect as soon as it is used – when you say it with full faith and congruency, you will be able to see the almost magical effect it has on you. Try it and you'll realise it works.

On the other hand, a regular use of 'cancel cancel' will make you aware of the common use of negative words in your usage. If you are like most people, you will be used to employing a number of negatives in your speech on a regular basis. However, with the use of 'cancel cancel' you will be able to make a drastic reduction in the use of such words. All you need to do is try it out!

How it works

The working of Jai Reiki can best be described by the process of anchoring in NLP. When you use the word, you are actually creating a mental association that tells your mind that whenever you use this word, you need energy. Of course, a lot of it is on faith too, but it is like a trigger word, a mantra that you can chant to invoke the supreme energy of Reiki.

'Cancel cancel' also works at the mental level. Your subconscious mind is like a field where you plant seeds of positive and negative thoughts. As you sow so shall you reap – that is the universal rule. But remember that you reap manifold. Over 90% of our thoughts are negative – and you can see that we manifest this in life.

Everything is created twice – the first time in the mind and then in reality. When you speak of something negative too, you are creating a picture of that in your mind's eye. Of course, it is a totally different thing that you don't actually want it to happen. But your innocent subconscious mind manifests all that you visualise intensely. So when you use something negative, your mind visualises it and it comes to pass. 'Cancel cancel' is a warning message to your mind to stop such imagery instantly.

Exercises

1. ***The ten-day mental diet.*** Go on a ten-day mental diet – for ten consecutive days you will NOT speak a single negative word and eliminate the use of any disempowering vocabulary. This does not mean you make your conversation unnatural, but don't use any self-defeating words. If you are caught saying something like that, you need to perform a constructive punishment, like putting some money in a savings box or anything that has a short-term pinch coupled with a long-term gain.

2. ***Catch the cancel game.*** When some other person speaks negative words, you can use 'cancel cancel' before him and get the points! The aim here is to enrol a partner in your commitment to speak only positive language. If you can do this, you will see the results improve even dramatically.

3. ***The Jai Reiki Journal.*** Keep a journal to record when you used the mantra and what result it produced. This will act like a scorecard for you and ensure you know what exact mental states you need to experience to make your mantra most powerful for you. Since each one of us is different in so many ways, the changes will have to be discovered by you so that you adopt this method.

EXPERIENCE JOURNAL

Tool Name:

_____

Possible situations where you can apply it:

_____

_____

_____

_____

My experiences with the Power Tool:

Date	Situation	Experience

Improvements that need to be made in my approach:

_____

_____

_____

_____

13

The Reiki Prayer

What is it?

One thing that strikes me in workshops I attend is that the Reiki prayer is skipped many times. When asked about the prayer, all that the practitioners can come up with is a puzzled look. This is surprising because something as holy as Reiki should never be done without a prayer.

The Reiki prayer is a set of sentences that you say with full devotion and in the most sincere and heartfelt manner. It is the perfect way to start the Reiki session.

How to use

At the start of your Reiki session, make the patient lie down and close his eyes. Since a part of your prayer is going to be for the patient too, let him close his eyes and experience the effects of the prayer.

You must also close your eyes and take a deep breath. Join your hands if you want, else keep them cupped in your lap facing skywards.

The three mandatory sentences of the Reiki prayer are:

"I am grateful to Reiki the medium."

Since we all acknowledge Reiki as one of the supreme energies that come to us in the hour of our need, we thank it first. This gratitude is expressed to Reiki energy itself, with which you will communicate more and more as you go higher.

"I am grateful to myself for learning this technique."

Next comes the person giving Reiki, which is you. When you express gratitude to yourself, it is an act of self-love that your body will respond to immediately. You will feel much better, because it is very rare that we actually acknowledge ourselves. This we must do before we start the session every time, for maximising the effect of Reiki.

"I am grateful to _____ (patient's name) for giving me an opportunity to use Reiki."

This is to express gratitude to the person who is actually not only a receiver but also giving you an opportunity to be a giver. The act of giving itself being divine, it is only because of the person receiving Reiki that you are getting this opportunity. Expressing gratitude to the person you are giving Reiki to will not only make it flow better but also give you an insurance against anything negative happening. You can't harm someone you are grateful to and, at the same time, Reiki can't be used for manipulative purposes.

The other sentences you may include in your Reiki prayer are:

"I am complete. I am whole."

This sentence is an affirmation that says that you are at the level where you can actually give Reiki to the person receiving it. To be healed is to be whole. So the affirmation "I am whole" affirms that you are completely healed. This

93

is essential since you need to be completely healed when giving Reiki effectively; results have been better when healthy individuals give Reiki. The simple reason for this is that when you are not fine, you yourself absorb a lot of Reiki.

"Nothing but only good things, love and light shall come to me. Nothing but only good things, love and light shall pass through me."

To affirm this is basically another request to the Divine that you encounter only positivity in your entire experience of Reiki. When you can encounter many negative vibrations and entities, this affirmation makes sure that you are safeguarded against any problem that might spring up. On the other hand, this ensures no negativity is passed on, either consciously or subconsciously to the person concerned as well.

"I invoke the Divine Energy of Reiki and request it to flow through me."

A direct invitation to the energy often works for many – when you ask you will receive. In making this statement as part of your prayer, you are requesting Reiki energy itself to assist you. Imagine the energy as an entity to be appeased, and you will see the wonderful effects that can spring forth.

"I request Reiki energy to completely heal _____'s (patient's name) _____ (part on which Reiki is being given) here and now, right now."

At every part that you are giving Reiki, use this sentence after the symbols are done. This will further improve the flow of Reiki. For instance, *I request Reiki energy to completely heal Hemang's heart chakra here and now, right now.*

When to use

Whenever you sit to give Reiki, whether direct or distant, do not forget to use the Reiki prayer. In our experiments, it stands out as one of the most powerful verbal tools. Participants have often reported dramatic results by the simple use of prayer. No doubt it is presented as an altogether separate power tool.

Effects and changes

The prayer works on two levels. The first important and profound but often indirect result is the change that happens to you. To pray is one of the most powerful gifts that mankind has – and when you pray you are talking to God Himself. Who would like to lose this opportunity?

Over time as you use Reiki, you develop a sort of emotional bond with the Reiki energy – when you communicate with it, you will feel it in your heart. For most of us who are living at the level of the heart, this is a wonderful feeling. It also increases your faith in the power of Reiki and makes you a more powerful healer.

On the other hand, the patient who is receiving Reiki will experience more comfort and relief, for now you have a partner in your healing and that partner is none other than Reiki energy itself.

How it works

The power of man lies within. Deep within us are powers that would astonish us, if aroused and awakened. Prayer is all about faith. The object of faith does not matter here – what counts is your faith itself. You can have faith in any person, object or abstract concept – it will work if and only if you have a feeling of surrender and a pure heart. So many great people have used the power of prayer.

For me, prayer represents the ultimate power that is – the power to talk to God Himself! Try it out, it works!

Exercises

1. Make prayer a part of your daily life – day in and day out, you should pray to the higher power. Don't miss any opportunity you have – be it travelling or waiting in a queue, the smallest of opportunities should be converted into prayer sessions and opportunities to turn inwards.

2. Prayers of gratitude – whenever you meet someone you know or feel for, pray for the person/group of people. One of the best gifts you can give is the gift of prayer; at the same time, it will make your heart more compassionate too.

EXPERIENCE JOURNAL

Tool Name:

Possible situations where you can apply it:

My experiences with the Power Tool:

Date	Situation	Experience

Improvements that need to be made in my approach:

PHYSICAL TOOLS

14. Salt-water Bath
15. Tibetan Exercises
16. The Candle Process
17. Aura Cleansing
18. Motherly Touch

PHYSICAL TOOLS

The mind first, then the spirit and, finally, the body. Any approach would cease to be holistic if it did not cover the body aspect of things.

Physical tools are really simple – they don't need to be explained or understood, but just done. When you do the exercises you will see immediate effects too – so measurable results become one of the prime benefits of the physical tools.

Start right away by practising the physical power tools. Because after all it's body to body, soul to soul.

14

Salt-water Bath

What is it?

Salt-water bath is one of the most instant and rejuvenating tools you can use. The concept of salt-water baths exists in a number of therapies, from Pranic Healing to Hydrotherapy. Reiki adapts from this tradition, and salt-water bath is a recommended tool for both, the practitioner as well as the patient.

How to use

Before you take your regular bath, just bathe with salt water.

You will need a small bucket of water.

Dissolve salt crystals (not normal salt but salt CRYSTALS) into the water. If you can't get salt crystals in the market, dissolve normal salt in water and put it to dry in sunlight – salt will crystallise and can then be used.

Having done this, you must take a bath with this salt water. The intention is to use it like medicinal water that is just meant to touch each part, but not cleanse per se.

After you have done this, you can proceed with the normal bath.

You have the choice of using lukewarm or cold water, but *don't* ever use HOT water.

When to use

You don't need to take a bath with salt water daily, though many of our participants have done that and are benefiting from it.

We recommend salt-water bath once a week when you're in perfect health. Else when you are under a healing crisis or some disease, you may even take the salt-water bath more than once.

How it works

It just works! There is no scientific evidence about salt crystals, because there is no concept of subtle energy out here. But traditionally, salt crystals are said to absorb negative energy.

Let us clarify that by energy we mean the vibrations or subtle energy of the place. Reiki is pure and neutral energy. However, negative emotions, events and people generate negative vibrations that affect the place and the productivity of the people living there too.

Salt crystals are even used for Feng Shui, a witness to the fact that a majority of the traditions subscribe to the energy cleansing theory.

Effects and changes

Salt-water baths definitely improve energy levels. One of the best ways is to do local application of salt water. Personally, when I faced a healing crisis in Reiki, I used salt water for my chest congestion – with often instant and wonderful results.

Another positive impact is the boosting of immunity levels. Any disease, before it comes on the physical body, manifests itself on the aura or the subtle body. What a salt-water bath does is work on this very subtle body. Often, the energy of the disease is cleansed there itself.

Finally, one more positive benefit is to cleanse your own negative energy. Most of us generate negative energy when we experience negative emotions, and this is what results in subsequent stress and disorders. A number of problems in our relationships are also because of this only.

Exercises

1. Whenever you have a chance to visit the seashore, do not forget to take a salt-water bath. You will return rejuvenated.

2. Disposing of the salt water that you've taken bath with is very important, since it contains negative energy – so it is best washed down the drain. Never water any plant or use it for further cleansing.

3. Put salt crystals, either directly or dissolved in water, at all corners of your room and check the results.

EXPERIENCE JOURNAL

Tool Name:

_____

Possible situations where you can apply it:

_____

_____

_____

My experiences with the Power Tool:

Date	Situation	Experience

Improvements that need to be made in my approach:

_____

_____

_____

15

Tibetan Exercises

What is it?

Legend has it that the monks of Tibet, who were practitioners of Reiki, used to do a number of exercises and postures to achieve vitality, health and warmth in the cold climate. The name Tibetan Exercises comes from this.

Most of the exercises, however, would be the ones that you must have already tried out some time or the other. But these have been specially chosen since they are the most effective amongst the exercises that are around today.

Tibetan exercises are a wonderful way to not only remain in the pink of health but also to ensure that the flow of Reiki from your body is at its best. Similarly, do encourage your patients to practise these too, unless they are prevented from practising these exercises due to some disease.

How to use

The following Tibetan exercises are to be performed as an entire set in the given sequence very slowly.

The aim should be to enjoy each and every movement instead of rushing through the exercises.

Eyeball rotation

Start with the rotation of eyeballs – begin by looking to the extreme left, basically as left as you can. Then look up, as high as you can *without moving your head from its initial position.* Then move to look rightwards – as far right as you can.

Finally look downwards, again keeping your head at its initial position only.

Now what you've just done is completed the eye circle. Next, move your eyeballs in this circular fashion ten times. Then reverse the process, doing it anticlockwise.

Neck rotation

Very slowly, rotate your head by looking left and then right and repeat this a few times very slowly, because the chances are that your head could be sprained when jerked. Now do that with the up and down movement. Once that is done, slowly begin to rotate your head in the clockwise direction. You may again do up to ten rotations and then do it anticlockwise.

Shoulder rotation

Keeping your hands close and glued to your body, rotate your shoulders backwards ten times. Having done this, do the same movement forward ten times. This is mainly to exercise your shoulders, which are affected by your faulty posture.

Elbow rotation

Make your hands into a lotus or a closed rose body – bring all your fingers together and having done that, take them to your shoulders. Repeat the shoulder rotation again.

Now free your hands and rotate them at the elbows. This would look like a dance step, but as long as it gives relief to your elbows, who cares! Don't forget to do at least ten clockwise and anticlockwise movements.

Wrist rotation

Take your hands straight and parallel to the ground and clench your fist and start rotation – first clockwise and then anticlockwise – of both the wrists together, and do this very slowly.

Waist rotation

Now you need to put both your hands on the waist – and start slowly rotating the waist from the clockwise direction first. Keep your head fixed or you'll start moving your body.

Knee rotation

Bend down a bit so that both your palms are on the knees, which are joined together. Now slowly start rotating your knees in the clockwise direction ten times and then ten times in the anticlockwise direction.

Ankle rotation

One by one take each ankle and rotate in the clockwise and anticlockwise direction. Repeat with the other ankle slowly ten times.

Typing fingers

Release your fingers and move them as if you're typing something with them.

When to use

Tibetan exercises are to be done every morning. You can do it whenever you have the time, but the best time for the maximum results is very early in the morning. This is the time when your body is full of energy. The next best time is after your afternoon siesta – somewhere around 5 p.m. or a little earlier. Never do these exercises after having a heavy meal.

Just before you start giving Reiki, you can do these exercises for yourself and for your patient too.

How it works

The mind and the body are inseparably connected, a fact now recognised even by scientists. When there is a change in your body, a corresponding change happens in the mind and vice versa. Given the fact that our daily life affords us ample opportunities to exercise the mind, to keep things in balance we must exercise our body too.

This kind of exercise opens up the energy channels. The best way to verify that this works is by actually trying it out.

Effects and changes

Most noticeable effects will be in the overall vitality and the energy level of a person, which will respond to such changes.

Apart from this you will notice that your own health and healing powers increase – after all, the healer has to be both fit in body as well as the mind.

EXPERIENCE JOURNAL

Tool Name:

_____

Possible situations where you can apply it:

_____

_____

_____

My experiences with the Power Tool:

Date	Situation	Experience

Improvements that need to be made in my approach:

_____

_____

_____

16

The Candle Process

What is it?

The use of candles merely represents the convenient utilisation of the fire element for energy. The universal life-force energy, i.e. Reiki, can be channelled and transferred using any of the elements.

The candle process is a wonderful way to give distant Reiki to a person. It can be used for "storage" of Reiki as well, just like a battery cell stores electrical charge.

How to use

Take a medium-sized candle (depending on how long you wish to give Reiki).

Hold the candle at the centre.

Imagine that the centre of the candle corresponds to the heart chakra of the person.

Now apply any oil on the candle. The application starts from the centre and goes upwards first. Then it starts from the centre and moves downwards, in a circular motion.

Then mentally express gratitude to the person and say the Reiki prayer.

Holding the candle, draw symbols on the candle (generally taught in Reiki II).

The name of the symbol is said at the base of the candle. Do this thrice.

After drawing all the symbols, light the candle when required.

This way you energise and programme the candle well in advance.

When to use

The applications are only limited by your imagination:

If you have an interview, energise a candle and ask a responsible person to light it during the time of the interview.

Similarly, when a family member is depressed or unwell, you can energise 21 candles at your convenience and light one each day. Check the changes after 21 days.

It is a wonderful tool for exams – you can help students by energising the candles well in advance, and they can light one candle when their exam commences.

Likewise, if you are ill, energising a candle, lighting it and then sleeping is a wonderful way to keep receiving energy.

How it works

Again, energy moves with intention. When you energise the candle, you're using the power of intention to direct the flow of energy.

The reason we need the candle is because our ability to direct energy is not at a level where it can "just happen". It requires something concrete to focus on.

Effects and changes

We have seen positive effects of the candle process every time we've used it. The effect is almost as if the person is receiving Reiki. Again, you will have to experience it yourself to believe in it.

Exercises

You can experiment with the candle process yourself. Light a candle just when you sit for Reiki practice or meditation and notice the effects.

If you're interested in exploring this area further, do read books about this. It is a part of the science of wicca – where experimenting with the types of candles, the colours, the oil and the prayer can all yield different results.

Remember to keep the candle in a safe place so that it isn't extinguished till entirely used up.

Also remember to use one candle per person per situation you want to give Reiki. Since each candle is uniquely energised, the effect can be different if this is not followed.

EXPERIENCE JOURNAL

Tool Name:

_____

Possible situations where you can apply it:

_____

_____

_____

_____

My experiences with the Power Tool:

Date	Situation	Experience

Improvements that need to be made in my approach:

_____

_____

_____

_____

17

Aura Cleansing

What is it?

An etheric body called the aura lies around your physical body. You have seven levels in all. The aura has colours depending on the person and his or her current mental state. It also changes in colour and size – when you're feeling warm and loving or blissful, your aura will expand. This is why you feel connected to things around you when you are blissfully happy.

On the other hand, when you're angry or depressed, that emotion changes your aura. Its colours too change from blues to reds as you encounter negativity. This is what we refer to as the "vibes" of a person. The reason we like to be around some people, especially enlightened masters, is because of their aura.

Aura sweeping is a practice observed both in Reiki and Pranic healing systems. It is a powerful technique for disease prevention and energising.

How to use

This exercise takes not more than five minutes.

The person whose aura is to be cleansed should be made to stand in a comfortable place. You need a bowl of salt water (crystalline salt dissolved in water) nearby.

Before you start, imagine a layer of energy around the patient. What you will do is sweep this layer of energy with your hands. Start from the head and with cupped palms, do the sweeping action over the head, the face and the back of the head. Imagine your hand is collecting negative energy. Now dump this energy into the salt-water bowl.

Come to the neck and again use cupped palms and a sideways movement. Include the back of the body too, since aura cleansing is done in a 360-degree fashion.

Once you're done with the person, sweep your own hands and put the energy in the salt-water bowl.

Make the patient sit and relax in a comfortable position for some time.

When you're using it on a single part only, do the same with the part, but remember to use the same sweeping motion and do sweep your hands after it.

When to use

Aura cleansing is effective when the person cannot take a salt-water bath – which is another form of aura cleansing.

When a particular part is severely affected, aura cleansing before giving Reiki dramatically improves results. Consider a filled bowl. When you pour water into a filled bowl, it simply overflows. To be able to effectively fill the bowl, you need to empty it first. Likewise, aura cleansing is akin to emptying the negative energy and then filling the body with positive Reiki.

How it works

Before manifesting in your physical body, any disease always comes on your aura. All emotions, positive or negative, are visible on the aura. Kirlian photography is rapidly giving us new insights into the world of aura.

When you cleanse the aura, you're actually taking away negative energy that causes disease.

In a world where energy is an abstract concept, aura cleansing might seem funny. But if you believe in what you're doing, you will notice the difference.

What tantriks and sages with brooms practise is a form of aura cleansing. Similarly, the ritual of *nazar utarna* in India is nothing but aura cleansing. No wonder salt is used for it!

Effects and changes

The part of the body where aura cleansing is applied is very receptive to Reiki, and if you're sensitised to the flow of energy, you shall actually feel its flow towards that part of the body.

Full body aura cleansing is relaxing. Since Reiki energy is not given till then, it will not be very energising. So Reiki should only be given after aura cleansing.

Exercises and tips

Always pour the salt water down the toilet drain. DO NOT USE IT FOR ANY OTHER PURPOSE, such as watering plants, washing clothes, or bathing. It is charged with negative energy and MUST be disposed of immediately.

If salt water is not available, visualise a green flame on the ground into which you put your energy. At the end, remember to mentally extinguish it. Since energy moves with intention, this is equally effective, especially if done with faith.

Regular aura cleansing is a great way to stay healthy and you can do it once daily.

There is no limit to the number of times you do aura cleansing and it can be done more than once for someone who is ill. But overdoing it is meaningless and akin to taking a large number of baths in a day.

EXPERIENCE JOURNAL

Tool Name:

_____

Possible situations where you can apply it:

_____

_____

_____

_____

My experiences with the Power Tool:

Date	Situation	Experience

Improvements that need to be made in my approach:

_____ _____

_____

_____

_____

18

Motherly Touch

What is it?

As the name suggests, this power tool is nothing but a touch that's given with lots of love. It's a wonderful way to end a Reiki session and one that we strongly recommend.

How to use

After the Reiki session, do some palming. This involves rubbing your palms together for some time to generate enough warmth.

After this, give a gentle touch massage to the participant starting from the head, which is the motherly touch. Imagine you're a mother touching your baby and project love from your heart.

Do this to cover the entire body, in as many top-to-bottom sweeps as necessary.

When to use

Though you may use the motherly touch anytime to experience being loved and cared for, here we suggest its use immediately after the Reiki session.

How it works

The touch is a very important aspect of Reiki and has been found to be healing. Considering how little we touch and hug in our culture, you'll realise how much it is needed.

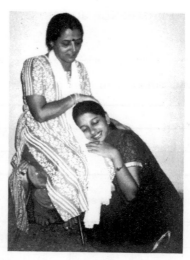

What a Reiki session typically does is energise a person and make him or her feel really great – like a perfect dessert topping after dinner.

Remember that love is the moving force of the world and your essential nature. When you project love with the motherly touch, you can actually catch a glimpse of the divine nature of all beings in the universe. Once you have tried it, you'll want a motherly touch at the end of every session.

Effects and changes

The entire feeling of the Reiki session is greatly enhanced by the motherly touch. There are participants who actually remind us to give the motherly touch!

It is a wonderful way to end the Reiki session, sharing the common love that binds us. It creates tremendous bonding between the patient and practitioner.

Exercises

If it is not possible to touch, you can do this at the aura level, i.e. up to six inches above the body.

Your mental state during the exercise is very important and provides meaning to the entire procedure.

EXPERIENCE JOURNAL

Tool Name:

_____

Possible situations where you can apply it:

_____

_____

_____

_____

My experiences with the Power Tool:

Date	Situation	Experience

Improvements that need to be made in my approach:

_____

_____

_____

_____

INTENTION TOOLS

19. Divine Reiki
20. Universal Bank Account

INTENTION TOOLS

What is Reiki without intention? The entire flow of the universal life force energy of Reiki is governed by the principles of intention and focus – when you use this focus in Reiki and hold the correct intention, the mind surprisingly responds!

In this section, the two tools presented are for the sincere believer of Reiki – not for the cynic who may scoff at them. With faith, even the strongest of mountains can be moved and it is with such unbending faith that you must use these tools.

19

Divine Reiki

What is it?

God is the ultimate source of energy – and, as most traditions lead us to believe, He is energy itself.

As our father in heaven, why wouldn't God be willing to assist us in our task? Of course, He would. This whole thought gave birth to the idea of Divine Reiki.

How to use

The use of Divine Reiki is very simple – all you need to do is that when you sit to heal yourself, you must have an intention of receiving energy from God. Whoever you believe in will be the source of Divine Reiki. Instead of taking water from the tap, you now move to the source itself – the Infinite.

It does not matter who the God is that you believe in – it could be a person, an animal or some object. It is your faith that is important.

Visualise this form before you. Picture as much detail as possible. And imagine energy being projected from this divine source to you as you give Reiki to your patient. It's as easy as that.

When to use

The use of this method depends solely on you – if you want to keep it as something exclusive, you should use it rarely. On the other hand, there are others who actually use it regularly with wonderful results. There is nothing that using it more would make it more effective or less effective.

How it works

Divine Reiki also works on faith – when you sincerely believe in a higher source, which really exists, it is a wonderful way to channel your belief. Also, it is much like asking for help when you need it. Ask and you shall receive, it is said.

An interesting story illustrates this point. A father and son were walking on the road and the son saw a huge stone in the middle. He decided to remove it and mustered all his strength. But the stone refused to budge. The more this kid tried, the harder the task seemed. Finally, he looked helplessly at his father – and asked him for help. The father immediately removed the stone with total ease and gently told his son, "If only you had asked before!"

This is exactly the principle on which the whole idea of Divine Reiki works – asking for energy when you need it.

Effects and changes

Many participants have reported a drastic change in their experience; many also encountered spiritual experiences using Divine Reiki. And yet, there were others for whom it brought no result whatsoever. The idea of sharing this is not to build your expectations at all – it is to encourage you to try this and see how it works for you.

You will notice that your faith in God increases, as you talk to Him more often. And that itself is a qualitative shift in our lives, as almost each one of us needs to get closer to the divinity within.

Exercises

1. When you are receiving Reiki, imagine the person giving you healing is a manifestation of God – your own belief will change the entire effect of the Reiki that you are receiving. When you can see God in your healer and really believe it, you are actually giving yourself more energy, as you know Reiki is more about being drawn than giving.

2. Give Reiki to God! It's a wonderful feeling to give back and you'll feel like a child giving his parents a birthday gift. Try it.

3. Regular prayer is a must. The best time is at the end of the day when you can reflect on how the day passed and talk to God about it. Have conversations with God!

EXPERIENCE JOURNAL

Tool Name:

_____

Possible situations where you can apply it:

_____

_____

_____

_____

My experiences with the Power Tool:

Date	Situation	Experience

Improvements that need to be made in my approach:

_____

_____

_____

_____

20

Universal Bank Account

What is it?

When you have excess money, what do you do with it? Having too much money when you don't need it may actually end up being harmful for you! So what can be done is simple – just deposit the money in a bank!

The universal bank account also works on similar lines – what you need to do is create a mental account that will be the place where you keep Reiki stored away. When you need it urgently, you can withdraw.

Before we get started on this entire idea, I'd like to make a few things clear – there are no units for measuring Reiki and it is more of a subtle energy force. How then, you will ask, does it get "stored" in a bank? We shall discuss this more in the *How it works* section. Till then, all I can say is that you need to have full faith in the entire idea. Check if it works for you. It has worked for every person who has approached it with faith, and yet failed each time a person has tried really hard but without faith.

How to use

When you don't have any body part in particular to give Reiki to, you can just sit down and close your eyes. Somewhere over your head, at any height and distance, visualise a sparkling silver crystal cube of any dimension you want.

This cube is your universal bank account. Mentally paint your name on it in bold in the colour that you desire. This will help you get a feeling of belonging to the bank.

Express your gratitude and sit in a relaxed posture with closed eyes. Now visualise the Reiki you're channelling flowing out of your palms. The palms are to be cupped and facing upwards for sending Reiki into the universal bank account. Visualise that the Reiki from your hands is flowing out in the form of brilliant white light. You may also alternatively visualise a golden light coming out. See that the light is going out in the bank account as you deposit it with Reiki.

As you give more and more Reiki, the brilliance of the bank will increase. This is nothing but your increasing bank balance.

When to use

Whenever you get time to give Reiki to the bank account, make it a point to deposit some Reiki in it.

When you need Reiki, you can mentally visualise the same brilliant account and imagine that you are drawing out of it.

If you are in one of your more philanthropic moods, you can also make use of the account to give Reiki to the world at large, or some community or group of people like cancer patients.

The whole impact of the thing will be different when the universal bank account is used.

How it works

The universal bank account being included in the Intention Tools section should tell you a lot about how it works. The whole moving force of this concept is its intention. What you are basically doing is collecting your intention – the mind being rational can't imagine the fact that you can actually channel intense amounts of Reiki at a time. But when you have some sort of a concept like a bank where you have deposited Reiki in the past, it makes sense to the mind, which is convinced.

Thus, the whole idea is to convince your rational brain with a concept that can't happen otherwise.

Effects and changes

Using the universal bank account is a wonderful way to channel Reiki energy and become a more powerful person and healer. When you have something like a bank account, you can actually make a good impact with Reiki.

Exercises

1. Every morning when you wake up, spare a few minutes to deposit energy in your universal bank account. This will ensure that there is a compounding effect and over the long term you will have deposited a large amount of Reiki in it.

2. Similarly, when you go to sleep or when you have time, do keep making deposits of Reiki in the bank.

3. Do not share this concept with people you feel will not agree with it. If it works for you, it works. Does anything else matter?

EXPERIENCE JOURNAL

Tool Name:

_____

Possible situations where you can apply it:

_____

_____

_____

_____

My experiences with the Power Tool:

Date	Situation	Experience

Improvements that need to be made in my approach:

_____

_____

_____

_____

THE FINAL TOOL

21. Learning

21

Learning

To me, there is no concept, no idea and no ability that is more fascinating than the ability to learn. As humans, we have been endowed with this wonderful ability to learn from all that happens. You can learn from anything and everything – from this book, from your neighbour, from the sky and trees and water, from the birds and from God.

Before we proceed further, I wish to present a chapter from my book, *The Portrait of a Super Student,* published by Pustak Mahal.

Keep Learning all the Time.

A Super Student is a student for life. In this dynamic world of today, change is the only constant. There is no way you can protect yourself against this. The only solution is to learn and adapt. Do you know why the HIV virus is so dangerous? Because it modifies itself to fight the antibodies that attack it. It is capable of mutation.

Similarly, to be invincible there is only one secret – and that is to keep learning all the time. There is no formula for success, but by making sure you learn, you will not lose the same way twice. As it is said, lose, but never feel like a loser. Whenever you encounter failure, ask yourself, "What can I learn from this?"

Feedback is the breakfast of champions. When you apply these techniques, a few will work. Others will require some fine-tuning, while some others may flop altogether! But what must you do? You must constantly see what is working and continue that. If something is not working, change it.

Remember, if you keep doing the same things, you'll get the same results. You must make changes as and when they are needed. If you can be flexible and adapt yourself, you will soon have a great bank of experience you can rely on.

Look around you – there are super students everywhere. After all someone has to be at the top. If it is not you, you need to find out what is wrong. How are the best students producing consistent results? What are their techniques and strategies? Make friends with them, and learn from them.

With life itself being such a dazzling variety, this book can't cover every individual case. But with this principle you'll attain the ability to apply this knowledge to all contexts.

The Japanese philosophy of Kaizen has caught on in management circles today. It means constant and never-ending improvement. You needn't be a manager to apply this – start today and keep learning. And you will be a super student all the time!!

Thus the attitude that you need to develop is the attitude of playing around with Reiki. When you can do that, you'll see the joy that comes in your life.

By playing around with Reiki, we are actually giving Reiki to any and every person and situation and, like children, just do it to see what happens. You need to put in infinite trust in this therapy, and it will pay you back handsomely. On the other hand, doubt it and it will be of little benefit to you.

The world of Reiki is filled with joy and positivity – but with these power tools, you will be able to explore this world better. Go ahead, the power is yours!

Epilogue

At the end of this wonderful journey, we take the opportunity to thank you for your time and patience in going through what we had to offer. We hope the tools in this book benefit you to the maximum and help you explore the wonderful world of Reiki in detail.

Before we part, we have a few final insights to share. Remember to use what works for you. There could be instances when some tools might not seem to work. What you need to do is keep modifying your approach till it begins to show results. Seek guidance from your teachers for this.

If something is not working for you, don't forcefully continue it – pick up only what works. Each one of us being different, you need to create your own customised course.

Always remember that the magic works with the person. It is not Reiki that is magical by itself – it is you who creates the magic. The magic HAS to happen to you before anyone else. And this holds true for any therapy, any faith and any path. The change you're seeking has to come from within.

Please feel free to ask us any questions, share your experiences and send us feedback on the book. We are working constantly at the Thakore Centre to develop more Power Tools for you. We are also working on having workshops for the same that shall be available soon. Till then, keep playing around with Reiki and experience the immense joy that it holds. Grow and be liberated!

Love and Light
–Usha and Abhishek Thakore
E-mail: *spiritualentity@softhome.net*

By the same author

The Portrait of a Super Student

—Abhishek Thakore

How best to perform in Studies, Sports & Co-curricular activities

Success today depends a lot on one's academic achievements. And to excel in studies, you don't have to be just an intelligent or brilliant student—but also one who knows how to manage studies and time. In fact even a mediocre or a below-average student can perform exceedingly well by following a scientific system.

The Portrait of a Super Student now brings you an innovative system specifically designed for super achievement. From simple, practical and time-tested tips on how to manage time, controlling temptation, scheduling time and work, relaxing techniques to diet control, speed reading, building vocabulary, improving presentation, discussing studies it goes on to guide how to make stress an ally, make a friend out of your TV and delaying gratification, besides others. And above all, to make it reader-friendly the book is divided into easy-to-read small chapters—with a practice section after every chapter.

Demy Size • Pages: 144 • Price: Rs. 80/- • Postage: Rs. 15/-

31 Mantras for Personality Development

—Abhishek Thakore

One tip a day to better yourself

Many of us have heard that the secret to a happy, joyous and successful life is to live in the present moment. Yet, acting out this simple truth eludes most of us. But the 31 practical tips and techniques in this book will teach you how to live each moment, each hour and each day to the fullest. By the simple expedient of making you follow one tip a day, each day the book takes you one step closer to becoming a better, more successful, happy and content human being.

Unlike other books on personal development and happiness, which are seemingly practical but not practicable, these steps can transform you into a new person within 31 days. All you have to do is read and practise just one tip everyday… beginning NOW!

And within a month, there will be a New You.

Demy Size • Pages: 104 • Price: Rs. 68/- • Postage: Rs. 15/-

The Practical Book of Reiki
—Mrs. Rashmi Sharma & Maharaj Krishan Sharma

Find balance and harmony in the mind and spirit. It is truly a gift to yourself!
Increase your vibratory level and healing capacity by treating yourself and others.
Be sure to engage your intuitive knowledge, feel free so that you can maintain the accelerated ability to channel the Reiki energy.
Remove the energy blocks and negative thoughts from Chakras and personality traits.
Apply Reiki by following the five principles:
❖ Just for today I will live with attitude of gratitude
❖ Just for today I will not worry
❖ Just for today I will not be angry
❖ Just for today I will do my work honestly
❖ Just for today I will show love and respect for every living thing.
This unique book is for those who are looking for a useful treatise for self-treatment and transformation with the principles of Reiki. It is a practical guide that tells you in a plain language to learn and practise Reiki—the Divine Universal Lifeforce Energy. Spend your day casuals in a series of moment-to-victories!

Big Size • Pages: 168 • Price: Rs. 108/- Postage: Rs. 15/-

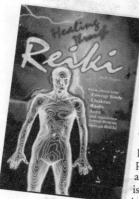

Healing Through Reiki
—M.K. Gupta

Contrary to what some people believe, Reiki is not a shady practice rooted in unfounded principles, but a systematic healing therapy based on the universal life force that pervades the entire cosmos. The Japanese refer to this invisible but universal energy as *Ki*, the Chinese as *Chi*, while Indians term it *prana*.

This energy forms an invisible pranic form around our physical body. This pranic form provides energy to the physical body and any disturbance in the pranic form affects our physical body, causing various ailments. Reiki is the science of tapping this pranic energy and using it to heal and nourish the physical body. Correcting any energy imbalance in the pranic form automatically heals the corresponding physical body.

In this book, the author highlights the association between the Japanese-discovered Reiki and the Indian healing techniques based on chakras, nadis and Yoga. Besides detailing the basic principles of Reiki, the book also outlines Reiki attunement or the process of empowerment. With many photos and illustrations, the book reveals Reiki treatment for specific ailments.

Demy Size • Pages: 102 • Price: Rs. 80/- • Postage: Rs. 15/-

Books on *Alternative Therapies & Hypnotism*

A.R. Hari
Magic Therapy of COLOURS
Holistic healing through colours

68/-

Rajendar Menen
The Healing Power of Mudras
The Yoga of the hands

80/-

Dr. Syed Arae Menerd, Dr. P.G. Sharma
Fruit and Vegetable JUICE THERAPY
Curative & preventive properties of fruits & vegetables in ensuring a healthy body & glowing skin

96/-

A Journey to Prosperity, Self-development & Transformation
Richer Life through Hypno Meditation
Dr Sanjay Mukerji

80/-

Gwydion O'Hara
The Magic of Aromatherapy

108/-

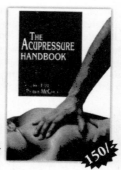

THE ACUPRESSURE HANDBOOK

150/-

Rajendar Menen
Magneto Therapy
The miraculous healing power

80/-

Rajendar Menen
The miracle of Music Therapy

80/-

A.R. Hari
WATER A Miracle Therapy
Global scientific research proves you can drink your way to good health with water

80/-

Postage Extra